LINDA RONSTADT
BIOGRAPHY

MEMOIR AND MUSICAL EVOLUTION

Jacob Jon Slyvan Miller

Memoir and Musical Evolution

LINDA RONSTADT

Biography

CONTENTS

INTRODUCTION

Linda Ronstadt, the legendary singer, crafts a compelling account of her upbringing in Tucson, Arizona, and her ascent to popularity in the Southern California music scene of the 1960s and 1970s in this biography.

Linda Ronstadt, whose forty-five-year career has included a wide range of musical styles, weaves together an enthralling account of her origins in Tucson, Arizona, and her ascent to popularity in the Southern California music scene of the 1960s and '70s.

Linda Ronstadt grew up in a musical family, listening to everything from Gilbert and Sullivan to Mexican folk music to jazz and opera. Her musical curiosity grew at a young age, and she and her brothers began performing their own music for anyone who would listen. Ronstadt now relates the narrative of her varied and entirely unique artistic path in this beautifully constructed book.

Ronstadt arrived in Los Angeles just as the folk rock movement was blossoming, laying the groundwork for the birth of country-rock. She helped create the musical style that dominated American music in the 1970s as a member of the coterie of like-minded artists that performed at the legendary Troubadour club in West Hollywood. Linda became the most successful female musician of the decade after one of her early backup bands became the Eagles. Ronstadt explores the colourful and interesting road that led to her long-lasting success in Simple Dreams, including the tales behind many of her renowned songs. And she says it all with a voice as lovely as the one that sang "Heart Like a Wheel": aching, delicate, and genuine.

CHAPTER 1

HART STREET

My home with Bobby and Malcolm was a little clapboard bungalow in Ocean Park, a community located between the Santa Monica and Venice Piers. The Santa Monica Pier had a stunning hand-carved fantasy horse carousel from the early twentieth century. In the absence of the flesh-and-blood variety, I would ride the wooden ones and fantasise. There was only a parking lot between our house and Santa Monica Beach's wild dunes. The neighbourhood was dotted with run-down Victorian seaside houses with low rentals.

The Troubadour is a nightclub in West Hollywood, roughly twenty minutes from our Santa Monica apartment. It was our first time performing in such a high-profile venue, and we were thrilled just to have the opportunity. Soon after, a man approached me in the Troubadour pub. I knew him as the proprietor of a nearby eatery. It was a fantastic restaurant, but we could never afford it. He invited me to his restaurant the following afternoon. He wanted to discuss business. I imagined he was interested in assisting us in purchasing equipment or obtaining a record deal. I rode the bus from the beach up Wilshire Boulevard the next day and walked the few blocks from the bus stop to the restaurant.

He was older than me, but he was still attractive, European, and had quite formal manners. In the empty restaurant, I sat across from him, and he got right to the point. He informed me that I was still very young, didn't appear to have a reliable source of income, was sure to face some difficult times ahead, and that he could make my life much easier. He'd pay for a good apartment, my clothes, and a sizable allowance of spending money. In exchange, I'd be expected to sleep with him. I was taken aback. I stammered that I couldn't see sleeping with someone other than for love. In addition, I thought I was doing well. I got paid to sing and lived at the beach with

Malcolm and Bobby in our awesome hippie crash pad. My mother continued to sew my garments on her sewing machine. He was kind as he accepted my refusal and we finished our talk.

I took the bus back to Santa Monica. I didn't know what to say to Kenny and Bobby, who were waiting at Hart Street to check if we were getting new amps. They were as surprised as I was when I told them what had transpired. No one we know thought about paying for sex during the free love period. He belonged to a different period.

The night we auditioned, another man contacted me at the Troubadour. Herb Cohen was his name. We had just exited the stage when he approached me and said he needed to talk. "Linda, this is an important man," a British comedian I knew said as he leaned between us. Take note of what he says." Herb grabbed my elbow and led me through the Troubadour bar to the restaurant next door. Bobby and Ken trailed behind.

Herb did not mince words. "I can get your girl singer a record deal," he remarked directly to Kimmel. I'm not familiar with the band." This remark made me angry. I thought I owed them my allegiance. I realised I wasn't ready to be a single act. We also didn't know anything about Herb. He indicated he could try to work out a contract with the band, but there were no guarantees. We told him we needed some time to discuss it. Herb had a reputation for being a rough guy, according to those who knew him.

Dick Rosmini, the guitarist I met in Tucson, was a well-known studio musician in Los Angeles. He was also a photographer and a commercial artist. He seemed to know a lot about the local music scene. Dick had shown up to our Troubadour gigs to take photographs, and he had continued to offer guidance and encouragement. We inquired as to what he knew about Herb. Dick described Herb as "complicated," but he liked him. Herb held strong political beliefs. He had fought alongside Fidel Castro in Cuba. He then became a soldier of fortune in Sudan. He then began supplying guns to Congolese insurgents. He'd bring a shipment of Algerian hashish to Paris, sell it, and use the proceeds to buy guns. The guns would then be smuggled back into the Congo.

He was in his Paris hotel one day, waiting to make a gun purchase with the proceeds from the hashish sale. His phone rang, and he answered it. "Leave" was the only thing he heard from the other end. He peeked out the window and saw the cops approaching the front door. Herb walked out the back door with the money in an empty suitcase. He bought a razor at the airport, shaved his beard, and boarded a plane bound for the United States. He arrived at Rosmini's residence with a suitcase full of cash and a great desire to work in a more secure environment. Herb utilised the proceeds from the gunrunning business to open the Unicorn, a folk music coffeehouse in Los Angeles. They were pals, and Lenny Bruce worked there on a regular basis. Judy Henske also worked there, and he eventually became her boss.

Judy was a beautiful brunette who was tall and intelligent. She was a chanteuse who sang blues and delivered hilarious anecdotes onstage. She had a nasty tongue. I met her at the Troubadour. She might have felt sorrow for me, sitting there looking neither hip nor savvy, because I had just arrived from Tucson. On the other hand, it could have been a fit of rage. "Honey," she screamed at the top of her lungs (Judy usually spoke loudly), "I'm going to tell you something." There are four sexes in this town: males, women, homosexuals, and female vocalists."

In the spirit of unity, I chose to accept her remark. It was quite useful information. We accepted a management contract with Herb when the temptation of a record deal and some coaching from a manager overshadowed Herb's unique reputation. I started to like him a lot. He'd settled down with a lovely wife and a young daughter whom he plainly cherished.

We went to see Tim Buckley at the Troubadour one night. Herb was standing at the door, counting all the clients who came in with a clicker. So the club owner couldn't refuse the artist's cut of the gate. Someone began to mock Tim. Herb took a ballpoint pen from his pocket and rammed it into the man's ribs, telling him it was a gun and pushing him out into the street. He returned inside, his sardonic, infectious chuckle still ringing in his ears. His strength was that even if he misled others, he never fooled himself.

He drove us to Hollywood's Capitol Records Tower, a famous "round" structure that resembles a stack of 45 records on a record player spindle. The elevator took us up to Nik Venet's office. Nik had agreed to produce us and had given us a standard recording contract to sign. Nik was a Capitol staff producer who had previously worked with the Beach Boys. He was quick-witted and engaging, more Las Vegas than the Ash Grove folk culture I thought I'd gone home to find. Musically, our band was quite young and hadn't grown much in the short time we'd been together. It was evident in the recordings we made. After our debut record was released in January 1967, Capitol sent us on a promotional tour of the folk club circuit that existed in the United States at the time. The clubs were crucial to the growth of music because they provided an entry-level environment for performers to learn and gain experience in front of audiences around the country. They also provided us the opportunity to hear performers from other cities and assess how we matched. That was extremely humbling. Detroit, Philadelphia, Boston, and New York were among the cities we visited. It was my first time visiting the East Coast. We opened for the Paul Butterfield Blues Band at New York's Greenwich Village's Cafe Au Go-Go. The air conditioner was more audible than we were.

After our debut record failed to sell, we began to plan material for a follow-up. Bobby's songs for us didn't seem like good vehicles for my voice, so I rejected them. Ken and Bobby had opposing ideas about the band's musical direction. I started looking for outside stuff. I discovered "Different Drum" on a bluegrass album sung by John Herald of the Greenbriar Boys and written by Mike Nesmith before joining the Monkees. I informed Venet that I believed it was a smash. We went into the studio and recorded an acoustic instrument arrangement with Kenny on mandolin. Venet was dissatisfied with it and stated that he intended to employ an outside arranger, Jimmy Bond, to recut it. I arrived at the studio a few days later and was astonished to see it packed with artists I'd never met before. Don Randi on harpsichord, Jimmy Gordon on drums, and Bond on bass were all excellent musicians. An acoustic guitar and some strings were also there. The arrangement was very different from what I had practised. I tried my hardest to sing it, but we just went through it twice, and I hadn't had time to master the new arrangement. I informed Venet that I didn't think we could utilise it because it wasn't how I had envisaged it. It also did not contain Bobby or Ken. He completely disregarded me. It was a big hit.

We were on our way to Hollywood for a meeting with Nik Venet and Jimmy Bond to discuss material and arrangements for a third album when we first heard "Different Drum" on the radio. We had run out of money. Our limited advances had already been spent to pay rent and expenses, as well as to fix Bobby's automobile, which was the only one among the three of us. It was still not working properly. Something froze in the engine somewhere in West L.A., and the automobile began its dying cry—a horrific sound of metal pushing against metal. We rode our screeching automobile several blocks down the street, turning heads. We got out and pushed it into a gas station until it eventually refused to move. The mechanic, who had heard us from a few blocks away, told us that the car, which had been laden with our guitars, Bobby's massive acoustic bass, and, most recently, ourselves, would never run again and could only be sold for scrap.

The jingle for KRLA, a Top Forty AM station in Los Angeles, came poorly from the station's garage. It was followed by a four-measure acoustic guitar-harpsichord introduction to "Different Drum," and then I sang. We were straining to hear it. We knew it was gaining attention in San Francisco, but we weren't sure if it would make it onto national playlists. Hearing that on KRLA meant it had happened.

Someone ultimately came to our aid, and when we arrived at Nik's office and began discussing our new recording, we found that being carless in L.A. wasn't our only issue. Capitol insisted on naming the new album Linda Ronstadt, Stone Poneys and Friends, Vol. III. They wanted me to take a strong lead so that I could be recognised as the lead singer. It was the beginning of the end for the Stone Poneys, not the beginning of their career. We began the tour in Utica, a college town in upstate New York, in March 1968. The audience tolerated us as the opening act, and the Doors members were courteous to us.

We had a performance in Boston the next day. We arrived at the airport early in the morning to discover that all flights had been grounded due to a huge snowstorm. Herb didn't want to lose money on a cancelled event, so we had to wait several hours while he rented a DC-3 passenger plane. However, we still need a pilot. Herb eventually located someone who flew in his spare time (he worked for a used tire firm) and was willing to take us there regardless of the weather. There was a lot of turbulence. We were all green with motion sickness, and it took us two and a half hours to get to Boston in a propeller plane. We had a day off in New York after Boston before playing the Fillmore East, a newly opened 2,400-seat venue run by soon-to-be-legendary rock event organiser Bill Graham. It was only his second performance at that location. The week prior, Big Brother and the Holding Company had officially opened it. Morrison and I had been conversing during the bumpy trip to Boston in the DC-3, and he asked if I wanted to spend some time with him on our free evening. Sober, he appeared kind and shy. I knew Bob Neuwirth would accompany us and felt he could keep him in check, so I consented. Neuwirth suggested we go see the Kweskin Jug Band, who were performing in New York.

CHAPTER 2

GOING SOLO

We returned to Los Angeles, with an unknown future ahead of us. Kenny quit the band and went to India. Bobby got a job hosting a concert series at McCabe's Guitar Shop, where we met Kenny for the first time. It was to be a very pleasant event for him that would linger for many years. Kenny later joined my backup band, and we recorded and toured together for many years. We all stayed buddies. They did, however, begin to share in the royalties generated by the sales of "Different Drum." I took on the debt on my own, and it would be eight years before I saw any money from record sales. Meanwhile, if I wanted to make a livelihood from music, I needed to get on the road. I had been largely a harmony vocalist in the Stone Poneys, so I was woefully unprepared to be a solo act. We'd relied on Kimmel to write the tunes, and I didn't have any of my own. I began to consider what I could do with the music I had enjoyed as a child in Tucson. The obvious solution was to play around with the 1950s country music I'd learnt from my sister's 45 collection and the jukeboxes in rural Arizona. Because they featured basic chord progressions, I began to play songs like Ray Price's "Crazy Arms" and Hank Williams' "I Can't Help It (If I'm Still In Love With You)" on my guitar. Herb believed I was wasting my time. He claimed that I'd be too country for rock stations and too rock for country stations. I ignored him and began looking for musicians that could perform Nashville-style songs with a California touch.

Clarence White, the poker-faced bluegrass flat-picker I liked in Tucson, had joined the Byrds and was playing a guitar he referred to as his B-Bender. He had built and fitted a mechanism on his Fender Telecaster with drummer Gene Parsons (no relation to Gram) that elevated the second string a whole step, making it sound like a pedal steel guitar. The lever that raised and lowered the string was attached to the guitar strap and was actuated by pressing down on the neck of the instrument. It established the California country rock sound.

13

When other guitarists learned about the device, they began to adapt it into their own techniques. Bernie Leadon was one of them. Bernie, a musician who has played bluegrass, folk music, and rock and roll, had the most musically integrated outlook of all the Troubadour pantheon's foundational country rock guitar players. He was a great player who had mastered a number of techniques while he was in his early twenties. He was also a steady, dependable individual who was more concerned with the quality of the music than with getting acknowledged. Players like that are necessary to any developing musical process and frequently make important contributions that go unnoticed because they lack the showboating gene. When he became a founding member of the Eagles, Bernie, like Clarence, became another pioneer of the country rock guitar style, one that had a strong influence on all of popular music. I first met him while he was in the Stone Poneys' psychedelic country folk band Hearts and Flowers. Before Chris Hillman joined the Byrds, he and Larry Murray were in the Scottsville Squirrel Barkers with Chris Hillman. Nik Venet hired Bernie and Larry to play on the Stone Poneys recordings after Hearts and Flowers was recorded on Capitol. Larry quit the band in 1969 to write for Johnny Cash's new music variety TV show, The Johnny Cash Show, and Bernie later became a member of the Flying Burrito Brothers with Chris and Gram Parsons. We hung out at the Troubadour and started jamming together, united by our ambition to fuse country music tunes and harmonies with a rock-and-roll rhythm section.

Herb found it quite easy to get me on television because I'd had a smash record. With its small displays and tinny speakers, I thought TV was a poor medium for music. In addition, artists had little control in how they were presented back then, and one would be asked to wear a costume designed by the program and colour coordinated to its sets. The musical director may also burden the music with complicated orchestral arrangements that do not reflect the artist's or the original recordings' style or mood. I went to Nashville in the spring of 1969 to play on The Johnny Cash Show.

I'd flown with a Herb's office employee who was in charge of getting me to Tennessee and making sure everything went smoothly once we were there. He evidently had more important things to accomplish and went on to Detroit after getting me settled at the motel.

The following years were trying. As a singer, I felt like I was floundering, and my style hadn't gelled. I opened for Jerry Jeff Walker at the Bitter End in Greenwich Village in 1969. Jerry Jeff, perhaps best remembered for penning the legendary "Mr. Bojangles," a song about an old street dancer he encountered in a New Orleans jail, was joined on stage by only one other guitarist, David Bromberg, a musician of varied genius and tremendous compassion. David is still one of my favourite songwriters, performers, and friends. I was charmed by his boyish, sincere earnestness even then. He approached me after the event and said I had to accompany him to the nearby Cafe Au Go-Go to hear his friend Gary White. He said White had written some terrific songs, and one in particular he thought would be ideal for me. I was expecting to be let down. I believed it would be impossible for someone else to understand what I was looking for in a song.

Gary was playing backing guitar for songwriter Paul Siebel at the Cafe Au Go-Go. We saw the last part of his very excellent show, which was enriched by his cowboy voice and a song about a heartbreaking, lonely girl named Louise, and then went backstage to meet Gary. He'd already packed his guitar, so he took it out of its case, sat down, and started singing "Long Long Time." I told Gary I needed to record it right away.

My producer at the time was Elliot Mazer, who later produced Neil Young's records and had previously worked with Jerry Jeff Walker, Gordon Lightfoot, Richie Havens, and Ian and Sylvia. He collaborated closely with Area Code 615, a Nashville-based studio band. The pedal steel player, Weldon Myrick, had an electrical gadget on his instrument that produced a sound he named the Goodlettsville String Quartet. It sounded like a gritty orchestra string section when coupled with Buddy Spicher's violin playing the top note of the chord. It had a unique sound for the period, with a powerful emotional undertone. The bassist, Norbert Putnam, rapidly constructed the arrangement. I think the musicians did an excellent job. I was never pleased with my performance on the record. It was recorded at 10 o'clock in the morning, which is unusual for a vocalist, and we used a live vocal. Later on, I improved my singing. In 1970, it was a great hit for me, and it allowed me time to learn.

I returned to New York to reunite with David, Gary, and Jerry Jeff and to record some new tunes. Eric Kaz was introduced to me, and he taught me a song he created with Libby Titus called "Love Has No Pride." We visited the hot spots in Greenwich Village at the time: the Dugout, Nobody's, and the Tin Angel. Paul Siebel performed once again at the Cafe Au Go-Go. We took Paul with us and spent the rest of the night performing music at Gary's small flat in the Village.

CHAPTER 3

CALIFORNIA COUNTRY ROCK

Back in Los Angeles, I kept looking for musicians who might like the new tunes I was discovering. I formed a band with Bernie Leadon and Jeff Hanna, who had recently left the Nitty Gritty Dirt Band. They were known as the Corvettes. We did a few performances across the country, then Jeff returned to the Dirt Band and Bernie joined the Flying Burrito Brothers. Bernie still played in my band when he wasn't with the Burrito Brothers, and we performed on a TV show called Playboy After Dark one night. We headed to the Troubadour after the show to check what was going on at the bar. Gram Parsons, Bernie's Burrito bandmate, happened to be nearby. He stated that he was going to the Chateau Marmont, a Hollywood hotel where he was staying, to perform some music. He invited us to join him. We climbed into Bernie's car and followed Gram up a winding road in the Hollywood Hills to a magnificent modern property that was not the Chateau Marmont. When we entered, we were greeted by Keith Richards. The Rolling Stones were in town wrapping up Let It Bleed, and Keith and Mick Jagger had rented a residence in Los Angeles for the duration of their stay.

Gram and Keith had become friends because of Keith's passion in learning about country music. We got right to work, singing all of the Merle Haggard songs we knew. Gram was singing lead, while Bernie and I provided harmony. Keith was jamming on his guitar and taking in everything Gram had to offer. This is how all good musicians learn from one another.

In the spring of 1970, I met two persons who would become crucial to me later at the Troubadour. One was David Geffen, my Hart Street acquaintance, Beverly Hillbillies TV writer Ron Pearlman's former college roommate. One evening, David introduced himself to me, and I found him to be just as Ron had described him, with a cheeky sense of humour and a restless, incisive mind. He had a kind demeanour, a private way of chatting, and an unyielding, seductive charisma. Elliot Roberts, a former William Morris mailroom coworker, and he became Troubadour regulars. As keen watchers, they established a management company and amassed a sizable stable of thoroughbreds. Laura Nyro, Joni Mitchell, Neil Young, Crosby, Stills, and Nash, and, later, Jackson Browne, the Eagles, and John David Souther were among them. David went on to found the extremely successful Asylum Records label.

John Boylan was the other individual. John was presented to me as the man who had produced Rick Nelson's most recent single, "She Belongs to Me." Among the Troubadour regulars, John was among the best of the grownups. He had thick grey hair and fading blue eyes as a young man in his twenties, confirming his Irish surname. He was intelligent, well-mannered, and well-educated, having graduated from Bard College with a degree in theatre arts. He understood his way around a stage as well as the music industry. He was in good shape, lean and fit. Fat John was his nickname. He made several recordings for me, and we began to form a travelling band.

I was living on Camrose Place with John David Souther, a little court of bungalows on the hill behind the Hollywood Bowl amphitheatre. He had the flint-eyed, dusty-wind squint of his Texas Panhandle upbringing. When I first met John David, he was drumming for Bo Diddley, but it was his songwriting that wowed me.

Jackson Browne resided next door in the cottage. Jackson was a couple of years younger than the rest of us, but he was always ahead of the pack. He was a little smarter, a little more evolved in his thoughts, and a little more refined in his writing practice in the Troubadour milieu of searing raw talent. He could make good use of his rather modest voice. Jackson uses a Doppler effect to begin a musical phrase that appears to be coming from a long distance at high speed. It increases in intensity until it fades out into the distance, leaving the listener dazed. When I met him on Hart Street, shortly after arriving in Los Angeles, he was sixteen, and he had already composed "These Days," a brilliantly structured song that ranks among his greatest.

I was beginning to feel the effects of time on the road with Herb Cohen as my manager. Herb was well-known for not spoiling his artists. He would tell me straight out when he believed I was acting inappropriately or exaggerating my own importance. Most musicians, especially female vocalists, can end up living comfortably at the centre of their own world, and I appreciate his efforts to curb this inclination, even if they weren't always effective. When he exasperatedly looked at me and said, "Linda, you're full of shit," he was generally correct. Unfortunately, he knew very little about music, and his great instincts did not include the capacity to even estimate what went into composing it. More concerning to me were his business procedures, which were somewhat unusual.

We had played a show in San Jose the night before we went to Hawaii, so the tickets we got from Herb's travel agency were for a flight leaving from San Francisco. We were fairly excited to go to Hawaii, and much more so to fly first class. We observed a few police policemen waiting close as we neared the boarding gate. They turned out to be interested in speaking with us. We were travelling with a fiddle musician, Gib Guilbeau, and I filled in on several of the songs. We both brought our instruments on the aeroplane to avoid having them damaged by baggage handlers. I was afraid the cops would suspect us of concealing weapons in our violin cases. I opened mine to demonstrate that it did, in fact, contain a violin, but that was not their business. Our tickets had been supplied to John by Herb's office, and when he delivered them to the guy at the boarding gate, they matched the numbers on tickets that had been reported stolen. We were arrested and taken straight to the San Mateo County Jail. It appeared amusing to all of us at first, and as long as I was with the rest of the band, I wasn't too concerned. Of course, as soon as we arrived at the jail, I was brought to a separate facility because I was the only female.

Herb and his wife had arrived a few days earlier and were already basking in the sun in Honolulu. Also, it was a Sunday, so no one was in his office. I phoned Herb's brother, Martin Cohen, at home and told him what had happened. He was a lawyer in charge of all of Herb's legal matters. It took him the better part of the day to locate a bail bondsman and get us out of there. I was chilly in the Levi's shorts and sandals I'd worn to the beach in Hawaii, and the jail matrons mocked my Porky Pig T-shirt. John and the band were in the drunk tank, which was even more crowded and menacing, but at least they were together. After we were bailed out, John drove us back to the airport and used his American Express card to purchase new first-class tickets.

When we arrived in Hawaii, we discovered that both the band Santana and singer Eric Burdon had been arrested for the same reason at different airports on the same day, and they had used the same travel agency. Herb stated that he hired that service because it provided him with substantial ticket discounts. He stated that he had no idea they had been stolen. I was curious as to what he planned to do with the difference between the money he received from Capitol and the price he paid for the hot tickets, but I didn't ask him. It was similar to how many people in the music industry operated. But I knew my father would never conduct business in this manner. It irritated me.

Cannonball Adderley and his brother, Nat, the jazz trumpeter and cornetist, were introduced to us in Hawaii. They were sympathetic to our stories of mistaken arrest and incarceration. I told John that I was unhappy with Herb's wrecking-ball management style, and he encouraged me to look for another management position.

Peter Asher and his wife, Betsy, had recently come to see me at the Bitter End in New York. Peter had extensive and varied commercial expertise, and he was one of the few people who understood both the music and the business. Peter, who was born in London, began his long career as a young actor in the British theatre, and he worked frequently both onstage and in cinema and television. He became hugely successful as one half of the duo Peter and Gordon, which he created with his school pal Gordon Waller, after his preadolescent time singing in a boys' choir. During the early days of the Beatles' fame, his sister, Jane Asher, became sweethearts with Paul McCartney, and Paul wrote four of Peter and Gordon's best singles, including "Woman" and "A World Without Love." When the Beatles decided to start their own record company, Apple Records, a few years later, they hired Peter to manage their A&R (Artists and Repertoire) department. He signed James Taylor to the label before leaving Apple and moving to the United States to become James' manager and producer.

Betsy was a good chef and a good listener. She and Peter threw wonderful dinner parties. Regulars at Peter and Betsy's intimate dinners included Jackson Browne, John Boylan, Carole King, James Taylor, Joni Mitchell, Don Henley, John David, and myself. Boylan advised me to ask Peter to manage me, and I informed Herb that I was terminating our working relationship. This was not going to be simple, given that I had just signed a five-year contract with him.

We recruited lawyers and endured a long and tedious deposition. Even though we were meant to be on different sides, Herb and I rolled our eyes and giggled with each other. We went to eat together during our lunch break, and he told me that the litigation would last forever and would be weighted in his favour because his brother was his lawyer, and his legal fees would be significantly less expensive than mine. "Linda," he insisted, "if we could just agree on a figure, it would save us from having to sit through boring depositions, and the money you'll end up paying to a lawyer could just go straight to me." We reached an agreement and shook hands. I had to pay him off over a few years, but we parted on good terms. I was disappointed because I actually liked Herb and still consider him one of the more interesting personalities I met in the music business, but I needed someone who understood music and handled business in a more gentlemanly manner. Peter Asher was a true gentleman.

John scheduled a meeting with Peter and accompanied me to ask him to handle me. Peter agreed to it. However, he invited me over to his house a few weeks later to tell me that because he had already promised to manage James's sister, singer Kate Taylor, managing me would create a conflict of interest that would be unjust to both of us—and so he would have to decline. I was disappointed, so I asked John, a record producer rather than a manager, to fill in until I could make new arrangements.

CHAPTER 4

THE EAGLES

One evening, John Boylan and I were recruiting artists for a Troubadour Hoot Night when a Texas band called Shiloh began to play and halted us in our tracks. They were performing my arrangement of "Silver Threads and Golden Needles," and they were excellent. The drummer, who was a solid player with a lean, unfussy style, impressed me. Even better, he seemed to understand country music's rhythm traditions, which encompassed the softer, unamplified sounds of bluegrass and old-time string band music. This was unusual for rock drummers, who frequently pounded over the delicate intricacies of traditional tunes and rhythms, emptying them of their allure. This made him great for accompanying a singer.

John introduced himself and asked if he wanted to play some upcoming shows at the Cellar Door, a club in Washington, D.C.'s Georgetown neighbourhood. Don Henley was the drummer's name. Bernie Leadon was booked with the Burrito Brothers, so I asked Glenn Frey, John David's Longbranch Pennywhistle companion, to come over and play guitar. We brought in a bassist and a lead guitarist, and Boylan performed keyboards.

We couldn't afford single rooms for everyone back then, so the guys had to share. Glenn ended himself rooming with Don and learnt why Don was so good at playing for singers. Don turned out to be a talented vocalist in his own right. He, like Glenn, was a talented songwriter, and the two began performing music all night, sparking a musical connection. Don was referred to as the "secret weapon" by Glenn, and they had chosen to start a band together.

John offered to assist them and suggested that they continue to tour with me while they waited for a record deal and their own engagements. They'd have an income, and I'd have a steady band for several months. Randy Meisner, according to John, should play bass. Randy had recently left Rick Nelson's Stone Canyon Band, and John thought he was a fantastic high-harmony singer and a good bass player. Bernie Leadon, another outstanding singer, was offered to play guitar. They clicked straight away and began working together.

They needed a place to practise their vocal parts one day. John David volunteered to let us use the living room of our small house on Camrose Place. We went to the movies to give them some space because their room was small. They sounded amazing when we strolled in a few hours later. They had worked up a four-part harmony arrangement of a song written by Bernie and Don and had spent some time perfecting their vocal blend. The music was big and rich in that small room, with only acoustic guitars and four incredibly powerful voices. The new song is titled "Witchy Woman." I was confident it would be a success.

CHAPTER 5

BEACHWOOD DRIVE

I moved into an apartment on North Beachwood Drive, near the Hollywood sign, with John David. We took it over from Warren Zevon and Tule, who needed space for their tiny child. It was in a wonderful Mediterranean building built in the 1920s, with enormous Palladian windows that let in plenty of California sunshine into our living room. John David and I resided on the top floor, and Bill Martin, a comedy writer who went on to have a long career as a TV writer and producer, lived directly below us. Bill coined the expression "The Whole Enchilada Marches On" when he wrote a profoundly philosophical song called "The Whole Enchilada Marches On." John David was an excellent listener. Hearing music with someone with a strongly shared sensibility boosts the enjoyment and learning experience tenfold. Years later, my record label's head feared I was wasting my career by trying to record "What's New" with a full orchestra and jazz band. John David recognized what I was pursuing and encouraged me. John David moved to a house a few blocks away after approximately a year and a half. We remained friends, but had become entangled in our own webs of needs and interests. He was writing a lot, and I was always on the go. We've always felt affection and sympathy for one another. I'm still curious about the tunes he's recently written.

My final gigs with the Eagles as my official backup band were at Disneyland in 1971 for Grad Night, a week of end-of-school-year festivities. We were on the same bill as Smokey Robinson and the Miracles, as well as the Staple Singers. The Disney Company paid much, but it had numerous specific requirements for the talent it hired for the park.

By late 1972, John Boylan had helped me create a solid following performing at colleges, but my records seemed to have reached an artistic and economic plateau. I was racing in two directions, one to please the record company and the other to please myself. I had tried to persuade Capitol to let me record "Heart Like a Wheel," but they saw no economic potential in it. They wanted me to collaborate with a country producer from Bakersfield. I believed some good records had come out of Bakersfield, particularly Merle Haggard's, but the style didn't seem to fit with my more eclectic tastes.

I only owed Capitol one more record. Other label executives were already making offers, including Clive Davis at Columbia, Mo Ostin at Warner Bros., and Albert Grossman at his new label, Bearsville. Grossman managed Bob Dylan's career as well as the careers of Peter, Paul, and Mary, the Band, and Janis Joplin. David Geffen's new company, Asylum Records, made the finest offer. It was a small label, and its few artists would receive individualised attention. Asylum was quickly becoming a home for singer-songwriters and the L.A. country rock sound, including Jackson Browne, Joni Mitchell, J. D. Souther, and Judee Sill, thanks to John's successful attempt to sign the Eagles. I knew I'd be in the company of other artists who shared my interests.

Geffen thought that if I released another record that wasn't properly pushed by a team that understood the direction I was attempting to take with my music, I'd lose the momentum I'd built. He suggested that I petition Capitol to let him have the next record, and then the one after that.

John set up a meeting with Bhaskar Menon, the president of Capitol at the time. Meeting Menon made me feel a little self-conscious. Herb Cohen had attempted unsuccessfully earlier to get me released from the Capitol. He had threatened Menon with bad public behaviour on my part that may reflect poorly on Capitol. It was a bluff, because I hadn't agreed to anything like that, and it was precisely Herb's artist-as-battering-ram management approach that had caused me to leave. He also urged me to consider Menon to be my adversary. I had never met him before and was shocked to find him to be a wonderful, polished, and intellectual Indian gentleman with impeccable manners. His delicate, gentle nature was a far cry from the cigar-chomping, hookers-and-cocaine-snorting American record industry males I'd come to associate with the genre. I sat calmly as my attorney, Lee Phillips, spoke on my behalf. Menon responded that they wanted to keep me on the label, but that I needed to decide whether to sing rock or country. I didn't want to make a decision. And I had a strong desire to sing "Heart Like a Wheel."

Menon didn't seem convinced by Lee Phillips's persuasive argument, so I decided to speak out for myself. "Please, Mr. Menon, let me go," I pleaded. I don't want to be here, I don't belong here, and you don't need me. Helen Reddy and Anne Murray, two additional female singers, are selling a lot of records for you. "Please let me go!" He eventually gave in, much to our astonishment. I had the option to sign with Geffen.

CHAPTER 6

NEIL YOUNG TOUR

David Geffen called John Boylan in January 1973 and asked me to be the opening act for Neil Young's next tour. To say the least, I was hesitant because my act and band were designed to play tiny clubs, and our first concert with Neil was scheduled to take place at Madison Square Garden. David and John recognized how much exposure to audiences throughout the country would help my album sales, so they talked me into it. We were headed to New York City with only a few days' notice.

That night, a few songs into Neil's concert, he received a message informing him that National Security Adviser Henry Kissinger had secured an agreement in Paris to cease the US participation in Vietnam. Neil simply stated, "The war is over." For the following ten minutes, the audience of eighteen thousand erupted, cheering, crying, and screaming. I was hunched in a corner in the midst of all the chaos, dealing with the fact that I was still a club act with a not-very-loud kind of folky band, no discernable stage patter, and no idea how to reach a crowd like that. For three months (seventy-eight gigs), I changed backup vocalists, stage outfits, and attitudes as we worked our way back west across the country. Every night, I was encouraged by Neil's piano player, Jack Nitzsche, who, in addition to being a great pianist, was also a terrible alcoholic. He informed me with metronomic regularity that I was not up to the task of opening for Neil as a vocalist and performer, and that he was going to talk Neil into hiring soul singer Claudia Lennear or singer-songwriter Jackie DeShannon to replace me. Even though I generally agreed with him, I wasn't going to let a drunk force me off the stage, so I kept looking for ways to get better. I also saw Neil, who was nothing but gracious to me, do his show every night, and I still regard him as one of the cleanest vocalists and most wonderfully creative songwriters in modern music. Hearing his uncanny, prairie-wind wail of a voice—a boy soprano pumped full of testosterone—in such frequent and intense doses was a significant part of my musical education and an ongoing delight.

The visit was taking place on a chartered Lockheed Electra turboprop plane. Assorted management, Neil's band, my band, and a few members of the sound crew were on board. Linda Keith, the stewardess, was married to Neil's pedal steel musician, Ben Keith. She handled her job cheerfully and efficiently, seemingly unaware of the chemicals lit or hoovered by some of the passengers during the flights. I appreciated that she also provided us with fresh fruit. She very likely rescued us from scurvy. We arrived at Houston Intercontinental Airport in late February. We were scheduled to perform at the Sam Houston Coliseum, a 10,000-seat hockey arena in Houston, with the following night off before continuing on to Kansas City, Missouri. When we arrived at the hotel, we ran with Eddie Tickner, Gram Parsons' manager. He told us that Gram and Emmylou Harris, the new female he was singing with, were performing at Liberty Hall, a well-known Houston honky-tonk.

Chris Hillman of the Byrds, subsequently Gram's bandmate in the Flying Burrito Brothers, told me one night that he and Gram had met Emmylou in Washington, D.C., and had fallen in love with her voice. He believed we needed to meet since we were exploring similar ideals in our music, and he was confident we would enjoy each other. I was eager to see what Chris had been raving about, so I asked John Boylan if he would make arrangements for the two of us to visit their concert after we finished ours that night. When we arrived at Liberty Hall, it was packed with members of the Sin City Boys club. They were somewhat raucous before Gram and Emmylou began to sing, but it quickly became extremely quiet. Something weird was clearly going on up on that stage, and we in the audience were transfixed. Emmy has the uncanny capacity to make each phrase of a song feel like a desperate plea for her life, or at the very least her sanity. There is no theatrics here; simply the sincerity of genuine feeling. The sacred beseeches the profane. My reaction was a little conflicted. First and foremost, I adored her exuberant singing. Second, she was, in my mind, accomplishing exactly what I was attempting to do, only much better. Then I made a split-second decision that would change how I listened to and loved music for the rest of my life. I reasoned that if I allowed myself to be envious of Emmy, listening to her would be uncomfortable, and I would deprive myself of the pleasure. I could take my proper position among the other drooling Emmylou admirers if I simply submitted to enjoying what she did, and then maybe, just maybe, I'd be able to sing with her.

I bowed out. Back at the motel, we informed Neil about the fantastic show. He and his band, the Stray Gators, as well as members of my band, joined us the next night. Gram and Emmy put on another fantastic performance, and Neil and I sat in at the conclusion. Gram and Emmy had received jackets with the phrase Sin City sewn on the back. One of the Sin City Boys approached the stage and handed me one. I wore it for several years. Following the performance, the proprietor of Liberty Hall had a party in the large dressing room upstairs.

That's when the trouble began. Jack Nitzsche approached me, placed his arm around me, and proceeded to laud me. Then his words grew increasingly aggressive. I wanted to get away from the nightly cycle of cutting remarks. Because he was a keyboard player, he had strong arms and a firm grasp on me. In his drunken state, he continued to slur the cruellest and most disrespectful things he could think of. I asked him to release me. He stated he was going to force me to fight my way out. It was clear to me that he intended to cause a commotion, and I didn't want a large argument with Jack to ruin the beautiful evening we had just enjoyed with Gram and Emmy. Still, his mean-spirited taunting had scared me, and I began to cry despite my best efforts. From across the room, John Boylan, Mickey McGee, and Ed Black, my pedal steel player, observed that I was unhappy and moved in to assist me. Nitzsche backed off with three stout men in my corner. We chose to return to the hotel. There were two or three limos waiting below. We climbed into the first one in line, where Gram and his wife, Gretchen, were already waiting. A knock on the window interrupted our progress away from the curb, and Jack stumbled into the front seat. He spun around and started talking through the divider. "You're a hot mess, Gram," he said. "You're fucked up." Gram's first thought was to ask aloud why the kettle was calling the pot such a dark colour. Jack persisted. "You're a drug addict, Gram." You're going to perish. "Danny Whitten's dead, and you're next," he added, referring to Crazy Horse musician Danny Whitten, who died of an overdose just three months prior. Gretchen began to cry. To silence Jack, Boylan reached forward and closed the partition.

Gram and Neil wanted to hear some more music, so we went to Neil's suite and started singing all the country songs we knew. Emmy was not present. We were playing old favourites like George Jones, Hank Williams, and Merle Haggard. Gram and Neil were performing some of their new material. We were having a good time until Jack strolled over to Neil's room and started bashing out gibberish chords. He then rose up and exclaimed, "Your music stinks!" "Let me show you what I think of your music!" He strolled to the centre of the room, unbuttoned his pants, and started peeing on the floor. Gram threw Jack's hat into the stream, and he ended up peeing in it. I was on my way out the door. John returned me to my room. I was fatigued and crying uncontrollably. A knock came on the door. Emmy was the name. She'd heard about what had occurred with Jack and had come over to console me. She gave me a yellow rose. I pressed the rose, and I still have it someplace in a box. Emmy is still with me.

Years later, when a period of sobriety had passed, Jack apologised to me. In retrospect, I believe he sincerely disliked my singing, and he was within his rights to do so. He'd have found me somewhat in accord, because I was still learning and, at first, totally over my head while struggling to perform in those massive arenas. It turned out that I was hardy enough to withstand his drunken comments every night. Jack was an incredible guitarist and arranger, having earlier written arrangements for Phil Spector ("River Deep, Mountain High" by Tina Turner) and the Rolling Stones ("You Can't Always Get What You Want"). What I found heartbreaking about his behaviour was that he denied himself the opportunity to function in the world with the grace and dignity of which he was perfectly capable.

Everyone boarded the plane the morning after the terrible episode in Neil's hotel room and pretended nothing had happened. Someone in Neil's group must have leaned on Jack and ordered him to get off my case, because he left me alone after that. The tour lasted another five weeks. I had a fantastic experience.

Gram died in a drug overdose six months later.

CHAPTER 7

EMMYLOU

I found out about Gram's death while driving, and my first thought was for Emmy. I wasn't sure what the link between her and Gram was like, but I knew it was strong. Anyone who had seen them sing together would not have questioned it. I called her and could tell by her voice that she was in a lot of pain. I inquired if she wanted to travel out to Los Angeles and spend some time with me. I had a week's booking at the Roxy, Hollywood's newest hot performing space and bar developed by Lou Adler and Elmer Valentine and co-owned by David Geffen, Peter Asher, and Elliot Roberts. I invited her to sit in on my show, hoping that it would pique Emmy's attention as a solo act without Gram.

When she came to my flat, the first thing she did was get out her guitar and play a song she had just written called "Boulder to Birmingham." It moved me to tears and established Emmy as a real songwriter. I was pleased to discover she had composed such an outstanding song, but I was saddened for her because of what had inspired it. We spent a few days looking over songs for the Roxy gigs that we could harmonise on. We wrote a couple of Hank Williams tunes, including "I Can't Help It (If I'm Still In Love With You")" and "Honky Tonkin'." Emmy taught me "The Sweetest Gift (A Mother's Smile)," an old song she remembered, and we transformed it into a duet. When she unzipped her suitcase, she showed me some garments that Nudie, the haute couture fashion designer to all of the major country and western music performers, had given her. Nudie and his stepson Manuel Cuevas, a renowned Mexican designer, designed the clothes Gram and the Flying Burrito Brothers wore on the cover of their debut album, The Gilded Palace of Sin. These outfits were jewels, but they were far too pricey for us to purchase. Emmy donned a pink Sweetheart of the Rodeo-style jacket, and she brought a red sparkling vest with white horseshoes on the front for me to wear. The sparkly vest was originally designed for country singer Gail Davies, and it came with matching short sparkly cuffs. They went with the Levi's shorts I wore to the San Mateo County Jail.

I don't recall much about the gigs we did at the Roxy, except that word spread quickly in Hollywood about the gorgeous brown-eyed girl with the burning ability who had been left wondering what in the world to do with her musical self after Gram Parsons' death. Emmy signed a recording contract with Warner Bros. Records not long after. The label teamed her up with Canadian producer Brian Ahern, who put together the Hot Band to accompany her. It featured some of Nashville's best musicians, including Glen D. Hardin from Elvis Presley's band, early rock-and-roll guitar hero James Burton, and composer Rodney Crowell. They created a number of fantastic records together, records that helped to establish country rock as a genuine musical genre.

Back on the road, we were performing in Atlanta when my band learned that a favourite band of theirs, Little Feat, was performing in a local bar. I vaguely remembered meeting Lowell George, their lead singer and primary songwriter, at my Topanga Canyon home. I'd never heard of the band. We went to see them after our performance, and when we got in, they were on stage playing "Dixie Chicken." Their Atlanta audience was enthralled. Little Feat, my favourite rock-and-roll band to this day, sounded like no other. Layers of bizarrely synced New Orleans parade beats were interspersed with Bill Payne pounding out a keyboard part reminiscent of Professor Longhair, Louis Gottschalk, and Claude Debussy. Lowell was soaring above this, playing slide guitar with an 11/16 socket wrench from Sears, Roebuck & Co. on his little finger. The socket wrench, which was heavier than the typical glass bottle top or lipstick tube used by blues musicians, gave him a languorous, creamy sound all his own. Lowell possessed a deep, amber-toned voice that he could whip into falsetto. His blues-infused vocal flourishes resembled classical Indian singing, and he had perfect pitch and rhythmic intelligence. His songwriting style was unconstrained by traditional pop music formats, with bizarre lyrics implying a tremendous intelligence.

Lowell approached me backstage, extended his fist to display a giant pill, blinked at me many times, and said, "Hi, want a Quaalude?" No, I wasn't looking for a Quaalude. I was curious about the open tuning to a song he sang on the broadcast about a truck driver. He referred to it as "Willin'." We all proceeded to someone's house for a long jam session, during which Lowell performed the song in open G tuning for me. We quickly noticed that my voice sounded best in the key of E. We promised to meet when we returned to L.A., and he would teach me how to play it in the new key.

Lowell arrived at my apartment with his large blond Guild acoustic guitar and taught me the song. One of the issues with changing a song's key is that the charm of the way the chords are spoken can be lost. Furthermore, having the strings relaxed, or slacked, to form the G chord adds some resonance to the G tune. The key of open E is not a slack key. Because the appropriate strings must be tuned higher to generate the chord, the sound is not as powerful. Nonetheless, the E tuning roared from that enormous Guild, which he left with me for a few weeks so I wouldn't have to return my own guitar every time I wanted to play the song. I played till my fingers were blistered.

I was in my hotel at the now-famous Watergate Hotel in Washington, D.C., a few nights before meeting Lowell, with a night off and nothing planned. The telephone rang. It was Emmy who called, saying she was spending the evening with a group of musicians she felt I had to meet and would I meet her at one of their homes. She provided me with the address and directions to a location in Bethesda, Maryland's suburbs. It was the residence of John Starling, an ear, nose, and throat specialist, and his wife, Fayssoux. When John wasn't removing tonsils in the operating room, he sang baritone in a bluegrass band called Seldom Scene. Fayssoux, a speech pathologist, was a stunning woman with a cameo profile and coppery hair down to her waist. She talked in the delicate tones of southern nobility, had a spotless home, and sang harmony even better. She, Emmy, and John had spent numerous evenings perfecting three-part arrangements to traditional tunes and country music standards, and when they sang together, they melded like family. There were two other members of the Seldom Scene: The banjo player was mathematician Ben Eldridge. Mike Auldridge, a graphic designer, played the dobro.

Most dobro players have a swagger and growl to their sound, but Mike was a one-of-a-kind. He approached the song with a deep devotion that gave his playing an unusually lyrical feel. His style was seminal, influencing many younger players, including contemporary dobro virtuoso Jerry Douglas. We sang and played late into the night, and the next evening I returned and we did it all over again. Emmy, who has an impeccable ear for a good song, was working on material for her major label debut, Pieces of the Sky. She sang Billy Sherrill's "Too Far Gone," Felice and Boudleaux Bryant's "Sleepless Nights," and the Stanley Brothers' "Angel Band," with John and Fayssoux harmonising beautifully. I couldn't wait to have another night off in D.C. to sing with them again.

CHAPTER 8

PETER ASHER

Kate Taylor was backstage at the Capitol Theatre in Passaic, New Jersey, where I was performing with the Eagles. For a time, we talked about knitting. She'd shown me how to knit woollen socks on five needles, and I'd told her about the heart pattern I'd drawn on graph paper and how exciting it was to see the socks take shape. After a time, she shifted the subject and told me she didn't want a singing career that required continual touring; she preferred to play music at home and not perform much. She persuaded me to re-ask Peter Asher to manage me, and she predicted that he would agree.

We were on our way to a staircase that would take us from the dressing rooms to the stage on the floor below, where the Eagles were getting ready to perform. I was looking at her face, making sure she was okay with what she had told me, and I wasn't paying attention to where I was going. I hooked my heel on the top step's edge and tobogganed all the way down. I'd had the wind knocked out of me, and while I lay in a heap attempting to collect my breath, I resolved to contact Peter as soon as I returned to L.A.

I called Peter's wife in California and told her what Kate had said to me. When I asked if Peter would still be interested in working with me, she stated it was conceivable. Why didn't I come over for supper and we could all talk about it? Betsy served us a casserole with pork medallions, onions, and potatoes, which we ate in front of the fire in their gorgeous Beverly Hills home's dining room. We had reached an understanding by the time we got to dessert. We didn't want a written contract. With a handshake and an embrace, we sealed the deal.

With Peter on board, John Boylan could return to doing what he enjoyed most: full-time record production. He became Epic Records' vice president of A&R and created a string of hits for a variety of performers. By the time Peter and I were able to record together, I had already completed Don't Cry Now for Asylum and was planning the album I owed Capitol. I hadn't performed "Heart Like a Wheel" for him because I couldn't handle the thought of the song being rejected again. I was rehearsing with Andrew Gold, the pianist and guitarist in my band, one night. During a pause, he started playing the entrance of "Heart Like a Wheel," and I started singing along with him. Peter thought it was a lovely tune. I added it to the program because Jackson Browne and I were co-billed to play Carnegie Hall the following night in New York City. It received a positive reception.

My financial goal for the next tour, which was set to begin in January 1974, was straightforward: I wanted to make enough money to buy a washing machine. Lugging big bags of filthy clothing to the Fluff 'n

Fold on the two days off before starting another tour was a chore, and I wished for a washing machine almost as much as I wished for a pony. The tour was three months long and featured Jackson Browne. We had our own bus but couldn't afford to have it customised with sleeping bunks and kitchenette. Ours had hard bench seats that were twisted around so that they faced each other. We could then play infinite poker games and listen to music together. We had a lot of overnight trips, so we went to the hardware shop and got plywood to bridge the chairs. We laid air mattresses on the board and made beds that were just slightly more comfortable than sitting up all night. We shared a bunk with two other people and climbed in wherever there was room. The air mattresses all leaked, so one of the two had to inflate them back up in the middle of the night.

David Lindley was accompanying us and playing with Jackson. David is a multi-instrumentalist who collects and plays instruments I can't even pronounce, let alone spell. He had enthusiastically explored a variety of different music traditions, including Middle Eastern and Central European, while still a young guy. David has an elastic face that, when it is at rest, settles into a puckish expression. He is one of the great musical characters, capable of changing accents and personas as easily as he changes instruments and music types. We discovered that our families are related through my grandmother's grandfather, making him my cousin, during one of our chats, with David Rolodexing through voices and personalities. I couldn't decide whether to feel pleased or disappointed.

David had found out how to sleep in the bus's overhead luggage rack after growing tired of the two-to-a-berth, leaking-air-mattress arrangement. This place was so cramped that it made a submarine bunk seem luxurious. He'd get up at weird hours and play the zydeco music of Louisiana accordionist Clifton Chenier at full volume all the way to the back of the bus. Nobody seemed to care. In the last stages of dementia, David was revered as a loving uncle.

Lowell George had a falling out with his bandmates and eventually joined us. He and Jackson sat in the front of the bus every night while Jackson worked on "Your Bright Baby Blues." Lowell played electric slide guitar, which he connected to a tiny battery-powered Pignose amplifier. On that journey, Lowell was also writing good songs. I recall seeing him write in a blank book with a Rapidograph pen, carefully printing in block letters the lyrics of "Long Distance Love" and "Roll On Through the Night."

We travelled east to New York City before returning south. Meanwhile, the 1974 flu epidemic was spreading among the passengers on our tour bus. That year, the virus was extremely vicious. Some of our band members were so sick that they had to be left behind because they were too weak to travel. I was coughing, sick, and unable to move by the time we arrived in Washington, D.C. That night, we had a gig at Georgetown University. Emmy and John Starling attended the performance. My temperature was taken by John. The temperature was 103 degrees. I sang nonetheless, but it sounded terrible, and I felt horrible for the audience who had to listen to it. John's wife had recently recovered from the same sickness. As a doctor, he was aware of how severe the virus may be and told me that it could lead to pneumonia. Lowell and I went to stay with John and Fayssoux while the tour continued without me. I missed the previous two shows. That meant there was no washing machine.

I went to sleep and didn't get out of bed for four or five days. When I eventually got up, I only had enough energy to go downstairs and lie in their living room's enormous orange leather beanbag chair. John put on his white coat and left in the morning to see patients and perform surgery. In the evening, he removed his coat, strapped on his guitar, and jammed with Emmylou and other members of the Seldom Scene. I could just sit in the beanbag chair and listen the first week since I was too unwell to sing. I began to participate in the second week.

Paul Craft, a composer friend of John's, drove over from Nashville, stayed in the Starlings' basement, and trained me to sing "Keep Me from Blowing Away." I decided to record it in Maryland with Paul and John playing on it. John recommended a competent sound engineer who had built a fantastic recording studio in neighbouring Silver Spring. He was brought over by John to meet me. His name was George Massenburg, and he would go on to become my most important musical collaborator, collaborating on at least sixteen albums with me.

Emmy arrived with her little pal Ricky Skaggs. He was just getting started as a formidable bluegrass tenor and excellent harmony vocalist. Emmy had met him through John Starling, who had recommended him for her support band. When I heard how well he sang, I couldn't believe it. I sat down with him and began to study. He taught me everything I know about bluegrass harmony over the next ten days.

Emmy brought over another acquaintance to stay in the Starlings' basement. Jet Thomas was the dean of freshmen at Harvard, as well as a proctor in Gram Parsons's dorm when Gran was a student there in the mid-1960s. Jet was modest and quiet, yet possessed piercing blue eyes and a sharp mind. Jet and Gram had maintained their friendship beyond Harvard, and Jet would periodically attend recording sessions and performances to lift Gram's spirits. Following Gram's death, Emmylou and Jet formed a strong friendship. Jet listened more than he spoke, but when he did speak, he had an exceptional capacity to clarify thoughts and shift attitudes for the better. He was a terrific individual to have around amid the M. C. Escher environment of the music business.

We played all the fantastic tunes we knew all night with such a great group of musicians gathered under one roof. It was snowing heavily outside. The snow was so deep by midnight that no one could leave. Great! We continued for several days. Emmy and I have frequently quipped that we have been recording music from our snow marathon for the past thirty years and counting. They've appeared on my records, Emmy's records, and the Trio records Emmy and I recorded with Dolly Parton—always with George Massenburg in the studio control room.

We drove to Silver Spring after the snow had melted and recorded "Keep Me from Blowing Away." Lowell went along to help and was so impressed with George Massenburg that he reconciled with Little Feat and convinced them to come to Maryland to record Feats Don't Fail Me Now. Long Time Gone is a wonderful album Lowell produced for John Starling, with Massenburg engineering on some pieces. Lowell persuaded Massenburg to relocate to Los Angeles, where he proceeded to record Little Feat as well as a string of hit albums with Earth, Wind, and Fire. He also created the Complex in West Los Angeles, where Peter Asher and I recorded for many years.

CHAPTER 9

HEART LIKE A WHEEL

In the spring of 1974, Peter and I began work on the record I owed Capitol at the Sound Factory in Hollywood. The fact that Capitol was able to claim that record proved to be one of the most fortunate breaks of my career. Al Coury, one of the best promotion men in the business, was Capitol's head of A&R and promotion. He sought to prove upstart David Geffen by running a better sales effort. It was also in Geffen's best interests for the album to sell because the subsequent record would revert back to him and sell more if the Capitol record did well. Both record labels ended up throwing everything they had at my project. I felt like a girl with two suitors vying for her hand in marriage.

I was thrilled to finally have the opportunity to record Anna McGarrigle's "Heart Like a Wheel." I put a lot of care and effort into planning the arrangement, which was masterfully written by violist David Campbell, and made sure there was a cello solo. I preferred the austere sound of a chamber group to the more lush, symphonic approach that I thought had cluttered up some of my prior recordings. During my floor-waxing frenzy in the Beachwood apartment, I also figured out my guitar arrangement for "It Doesn't Matter Anymore." Emmylou and I had been working on some harmonies for "I Can't Help It (If I'm Still In Love With You)," and she decided to fly out and record it with me.

Because I am mostly a ballad singer, I believe it is important to have uptempo songs on my records and in my concerts so that the audience does not fall asleep listening to one slow song after another. As an afterthought, I decided to include a song I'd been using to end our concert on the record. I had learned it at the recommendation of Stone Poneys bandmate Kenny Edwards from the singing of soul singer Betty Everett, widely known for her classic "The Shoop

Shoop Song (It's in His Kiss)." The song was named "You're No Good." We were bored with the arrangement we were employing onstage and decided to try something different. Ed Black, a six-string guitarist and pedal steel player, began to play a rhythm riff on his Les Paul. Kenny Edwards, who had recently joined the band as bassist, mimicked the riff in octaves. Andrew Gold contributed a sparse percussion part, providing me with a solid foundation to sing over.

We did a couple takes, chose one, and then Andrew, who also played guitars and keyboards, went to work with Peter, layering guitar, piano, and percussion sounds. They began to compose and piece together Andrew's guitar solo after several hours of adding to the core track. This was accomplished by recording many audio of Andrew playing the solo in various ways and then editing together the parts they liked best. They then added further layers of Andrew playing guitars with various electronic effects until the solo was complete. It took several hours more. When they finished putting together the solo, we all sat down to hear what had taken so long to put together, to see if it was as good as we believed it was. While they were working, I went out for an hour to eat dinner and returned with a friend. He remarked on the solo, perplexed as to why it suddenly sounded like the Beatles. Peter, who had worked so hard and was so pleased with the outcome, did not appear to be pleased. I requested to hear it again. Our engineer, Val Garay, had been sitting at the console all day and into the morning. He was exhausted. During replay, he sought for the track containing the composite guitar solo, but he pressed the wrong button, erasing the entire thing. When he understood what he'd done, his face turned putty grey. Peter maintained a deadly calm. I could see the gears working in his head, desperately trying to figure out how to reclaim what had been lost. Andrew opened his case, took out the guitar he'd just packed, and they began again. I went home and fell asleep. The next morning, I returned to the studio and listened to the repaired solo. Peter, Val, and Andrew were very exhausted. It sounded fantastic.

The single "You're No Good" was released. On the opposite side, we featured "I Can't Help It (If I'm Still In Love With You)," a duet I did with Emmylou Harris. "You're No Good" reached number one on the Billboard Hot 100 in February 1975. Furthermore, "I Can't Help It (If I'm Still In Love With You)" reached number two on the country chart.

CHAPTER 10

MALIBU

"Heart Like a Wheel" gave birth to two additional smash songs, "When Will I Be Loved" and "It Doesn't Matter Anymore." I now had enough money to purchase a washing machine. I started looking for a house to go with it. I had become an exercise enthusiast and desired to run in fresh air and soft sand. I bought a little Cape Cod-style beach house in Malibu, about twenty minutes north of Santa Monica, where I had resided during my Stone Poneys days. Adam Mitchell, a Canadian songwriter, has moved into the apartment above my garage. He was an excellent roommate. Adam created wonderful songs, was an outstanding guitarist, and had a pure, falsetto-infused vocal style with the Celtic flair of his native Scotland that I adored. When he was a child, his family moved from Scotland to Canada. After having his nose shattered by a hockey stick, he picked up a guitar and joined the Paupers, a successful Canadian rock band. He was also an avid runner. I was constantly touring, so having him reside there meant I had someone to look after my house while I was away. Adam required silence and privacy to work, and I had a piano available for him to use anytime he needed it.

Emmylou introduced me to Nicolette Larson, who was performing with Commander Cody and His Lost Planet Airmen, and we hit it off right away. Emmy and Nicolette had recorded a duet of "Hello Stranger," a Carter Family tune that had received a lot of playing on Country Radio. Nicky had a sincere, midwestern prairie-girl sweetness that could make even the most mundane task enjoyable. Her hair was gorgeous: thick and wavy and flowing over her waist. We exchanged clothes, bags, and our innermost romantic secrets. She would go to the beach and spend days there. We made cherry pies and whole wheat bread as Adam sang harmonies.

John David Souther and Don Henley resided a little further north of Malibu Colony and would pop by to play their new songs on occasion. It was like our days on Camrose Place when they'd bring in Jackson Browne or Glenn Frey. Neil Young approached me and asked me to perform harmonies on his album American Stars 'n Bars. That night, Nicolette was there, and he liked the way we sounded together, so we went to his magnificent ranch in Northern California and worked for several days. He referred to us as the Saddle Bags.

I first met Neil in 1971, when I was performing on The Johnny Cash Show for the second time, alongside Neil and James Taylor. The show was recorded at Nashville's Ryman Auditorium, which is famous for being the original home of the Grand Ole Opry. On one of our nights off, Earl Scruggs's teenage guitar wizard son, Randy, invited me to an Opry concert and introduced me to Dolly Parton. I recall thinking she had the most gorgeous skin I'd ever seen. She had an exuberant charm to match. I had heard her rendition of "Jolene," a song she had composed, and told her how much I enjoyed it. I also admired her enormous, puffy skirt, and she told me I shouldn't view of her as a stupid country girl because of how she dressed. I hadn't considered that, but I accepted her word for it.

After taping the Cash show all day, John Boylan and I headed down to Quadraphonic Studios, just south of Music Row, where Neil was recording Harvest. Neil had requested that James and I sing backup harmonies on "Heart of Gold" and "Old Man." James also strummed a six-string banjo tuned like a guitar. They wanted us to sing into the same microphone. This presented a challenge because I am short and James is very tall. He ended up sitting on a chair to accommodate his banjo playing, while I knelt alongside him, stretching to reach the mike and singing extremely high notes to obtain a harmony over James. This carried on for hours and hours till the next morning, with no complaints. When the music is good, you don't become bored or tired of it. One of the tracks we recorded that night, "Heart of Gold," became Neil's biggest single. We walked out of the studio into a chilly morning and a record-breaking snowstorm. It was pleasant for us.

Neil had a full recording studio at his property by the time we recorded Stars 'n Bars some years later. It includes an ancient tube mixing board from Hollywood's famed Gold Star Recording Studios, where producer Phil Spector recorded his "Wall of Sound" songs. Neil was a bit of a reactive in his recording manner, as I discovered during the Harvest sessions. Instead of recording a basic track and then overdubbing for days, Neil preferred to have everyone playing at the same time, giving his records an unmistakably raw, spontaneous feel. There is no single correct technique to record. It is a matter of personal preference. When I worked with Paul Simon on Graceland in the mid-1980s, he built his songs a few tracks at a time, layering sound the way the seventeenth-century Dutch painter Vermeer layered oil paint. Neil's art resembles a pen and ink drawing. Both of them are masters. Nicolette recorded Neil's song "Lotta Love" at my recommendation and scored her first solo hit. Ted Templeman, her producer, placed a fantastic sound system in my new Mercedes convertible as a thank you. I drove up and down Sunset Boulevard, from Pacific Coast Highway to Hollywood, playing Beach Boys music and loving the way salt crystals hung in the air, illuminating a rosy hue. Life was great.

I began working out with a personal trainer named Max Sikinger. He stood approximately five feet tall and was extremely knowledgeable about the intricacies of the human body. I discovered that he was the inspiration for Eden Ahbez's wonderful song "Nature Boy," which was sung by Nat "King" Cole in 1948 and which I have long admired. The song's description of Max is spot on.

Max was born in Germany and told me that when he was five years old, near the conclusion of World War I, he was in a train station with his mother when bombs began to explode. He never found his mother again ("a little shy, and sad of eye"). He was taken in by a group of street youths, his low stature most likely due to many years of near hunger in postwar Germany's rubble. He lied about his age and took a job on a merchant ship docked in New York when he was approximately fifteen. Max hopped ship and made his way across the country, eventually landing in Southern California. He was one of the early fitness advocates seen on Muscle Beach, a strip of sand south of the Santa Monica Pier, among musclemen like Jack LaLanne, Max Gold, and Steve Reeves. Max began training Mr. Universe contenders, and by the time I met him in the mid-1970s, he was training movie stars and teaching them about raw diets, juice fasts, and weight lifting. Now, gyms are packed with women lifting weights, but back then, Max's girls were the only ones. He taught me that a lengthy trip was a better therapy for depression than years of then-popular Freudian analysis or medicines, whether obtained legally or illegally.

I'm terribly allergic to alcohol and have never been able to stomach any amount of it. I tried to become drunk a few times by drinking tequila, my father's favourite drink. As a result, I had a bright red face and puked for several days. I never felt a buzz and instead experienced a severe hangover. Cocaine sent me to the doctor with a bloody nose that needed cauterization. My doctor enthusiastically explained to me while I was there that cocaine causes the cilia in the ear canal to lie down and many never get back up. This may result in irreversible hearing loss. My fascination with cocaine ended when I realised that my hearing was a vital element in my musical toolbox. Max had given me a strong body and a pleasant contrast to the music industry's drugs and carousing lifestyle. This was a very generous present. I acquired a dappled grey Arabian horse and attempted to recreate my childhood exploits, but riding through overdeveloped suburban Los Angeles was never the same as the wild freedom I had experienced in the Arizona desert with my childhood friend Dana and our horses, Murphy and Little Paint.

Nicolette showed up at the beach with a new set of roller skates one day. They weren't like the modern in-line Rollerblades or the creaky metal ones I used to have as a kid, which fit to my saddle shoes with a key hung on a ribbon around my neck. They were shoe skates with broad vinyl wheels that provided an amazingly smooth ride. It was like walking around with a Cadillac on each foot. Nicky and I began skating on Venice Beach, which we liked since it was full of outlandish individuals from Southern California. There were old

Jewish lefties playing chess, Beat Generation survivors, Muscle Beach bodybuilders, and street performers. There were also slackers and stoners of all kinds lounging around, enjoying the nice sun and the hot girls in skimpy outfits. Skating helped us break free from vehicle culture. If we saw anything we liked, we could pull over and join in without having to find a parking spot. We could leave if we didn't like what we saw.

We were both inexperienced skaters who could only stop by clutching a pole or a tree. We had a friend named Dan Blackburn who worked as an NBC news journalist. He was an excellent skater and offered to meet us at the beach to give us some pointers. Dan said he'd bring a friend he'd like us to meet.

He arrived on time and introduced us to a skinny brunette, quiet and attractive, with a polished, well-dressed demeanour. Leslie was her name. We skated for about an hour until we were approached by a swarm of people lying on the ground, grabbing our ankles and pleading for water. Some of them were chowing down on dirt. They were definitely squandered on something potent. Someone mentioned "angel dust," the street name for PCP. Angel dust's analgesic impact might keep users from noticing they need water, and by the time the medication wears off, they are desperate for water.

We got away and skated to a local restaurant for lunch. We started talking about how we felt terrible and embarrassed for the folks we saw, how they had been stripped of any dignity they may have had, and how angel dust seemed like a nasty drug after we ordered. Nicky and I had never tried it and were curious about its appeal. Quiet Leslie became excited and stated that, indeed, it was a very nasty drug that might compel one to do things they would never do sober. She claimed to know this because she had done some awful things when high on drugs and ended up in jail. I innocently inquired about her arrest, recalling my own time in jail. "Murder," she said.

"Well, who exactly did you murder?" Nicky mumbled.

Leslie responded by stating that her full name was Leslie Van Houten and that she was a member of Charles Manson's "family."

We were gagging on our burgers, Nicolette and I. She appeared to be kind and average. We respectfully inquired as to how she had gotten out of jail and was now lunching and roller skating with us rather than sitting in a cell with the rest of her companions. She was on appeal because her attorney went missing during the trial, and she was determined to have had ineffective assistance at trial. According to her, the combination of Charles Manson's influence and the drugs he pushed her to use would persuade the court that she was not in her right mind and thus innocent.

Dan and Leslie left us wondering how someone's life could go from normal to grotesquely sad in an instant. As we skated back to the car, we worried if this might happen to either of us. Or was it someone we cared about? It definitely bolstered the anti-drug hearing-loss argument. I was so upset and distracted that I lost track of what my feet were doing and landed hard on the concrete. This, combined with my tumble down the steps at the Capitol Theatre a few years previously, resulted in years of back pain. Leslie's appeal, predictably, was unsuccessful, as she was retried and ultimately found guilty. She was returned to prison after nearly a year of freedom, where she remains to this day.

My Malibu cottage's phone was ringing. It was Emmylou calling, saying she had Dolly Parton in her living room and asked me to come over. I rushed in my car, drove as fast as I could over the serpentine curves of Sunset Boulevard, and arrived at her house in Coldwater Canyon in record time. Emmy and Dolly were sitting on the couch, sharing stories and laughing. Emmy had her guitar out, and we started playing music right away. Dolly offered "Bury Me Beneath the Willow," a Carter Family classic, and we performed it in three-part harmony. The effect of our combined voices startled and stunned us all. Emmy and I had performed and sang with a wide range of artists, including Neil Young, Roy Orbison, George Jones, and Ricky Skaggs. Because we are all excellent singers and musicians, it sounded very decent overall. This new sound, on the other hand, was unique. We both appeared to discover it at the same time and instantly started looking for additional tunes to sing together.

There are many trio configurations for males in American traditional music, but not so many for women. Bluegrass singing has traditionally been a man's realm, and for good reason. The attempt to push the male harmonies so high—a wail one notch below a scream—gives the vocal blend an edge and tension, generating the "high, lonesome sound."

Women's harmonising styles appear to me to be no less urgent and far more contemplative. Both men and women toiled in the rural villages that provided us with our rich heritage of Americana music. Farming, mining, and building railways and bridges were all bone-crushing jobs for men. It was seven days a week of laundry, cleaning, kid care, and putting three meals on the table for women. I imagine them sitting in a neat parlour, sharing their troubles, joys, and disappointments with sisters or intimate friends when they did have time to steal away and perform music. They'd be playing whatever instruments and at whatever level of musical proficiency they could muster before returning to the never-ending task of running a household.

The music we were making was neither bluegrass nor honky-tonk country. It wasn't even limited to what Dolly called "old-timey music," as we wanted to explore more recently composed material like Kate and Anna McGarrigle's tunes, or Linda Thompson's LPs with her then-husband, British artist Richard Thompson. We came to think of it as "parlour music"—something more refined and elegant than bluegrass, honky-tonk, or the current pop music we heard on the radio.

We made the decision to make a record together. While the benefits of this concept were obvious to us, it was not so to our individual managers or record labels.

A number of attempts had been made to form and record "supergroups," which were made up of tremendously popular and easily identifiable names from diverse rock bands. Sometimes the music from these ensembles was good, and sometimes it wasn't. We weren't attempting to capitalise on the fact that we were three well-known names. We wanted to do it because we suspected musical affinity at the deepest level of instinct. Of course, juggling the conflicts and demands of three separate careers represented by separate managers, agents, and record labels made singing together professionally nearly impossible. We never did manage to align the planets for a concert tour, but we did manage to squeeze in enough time to record two albums throughout the years.

Musically, I found the experience quite rewarding, with everyone of us contributing something unique to the music. Emmy was always good at picking out the best songs. Dolly's Appalachian look, complete with ribbon-bow embellishments, added authenticity to the more traditional melodies. Dolly and Emmy are both natural harmony singers, but it was typically up to me to work out the more tricky harmony sections. We'd sing the songs in various vocal configurations, alternating who sang high or low harmonies and who sang lead, and then decide which sounded best for that particular song. We may also duet successfully as Emmy and I, Dolly and I, or Dolly and Emmy. My favourite way, which we utilised on "My Dear Companion," was for Emmy to start the lead, then have Dolly soaring above, dipping and gliding like a beautiful kite. I discovered that I could sing with them in ways that I couldn't accomplish by myself. I'm rarely happy listening to my own recordings since I always find something I should have done better, but the sound we generated together was very distinct from our individual sounds and could be listened to with a rare sense of objectivity.

By the time we figured out how to juggle three active occupations and launched Trio, it was 1987. When we initially started singing together in the mid-1970s, we attempted to make a record, but it was unsatisfactory and was never released. We individually choose our favourite tunes from those sessions and use them in our own projects. Nonetheless, we were determined to produce a full album of the three of us singing together. With Dolly in between recording contracts and Emmy and I both signed to Warner Bros. labels, it felt like a good time to resuscitate the notion. We chose George Massenburg to produce because he had demonstrated exceptional sensitivity to the recording needs of acoustic instruments while working with John Starling and the Seldom Scene. We immediately contacted Starling and asked him to come out and play guitar. Emmy and I had great faith in John's musical sense, so we asked him to help us create our vision for the trio's sound.

Emmylou arrived with an armload of great songs, as she always does. They were mostly traditional in style, but they did include the unexpected choice "To Know Him Is to Love Him," a 1958 classic penned by Phil Spector for the Teddy Bears. We recorded it with a band made up of great acoustic string band instrumentalists who Emmy and I had long admired and worked with. They included mandolinist Mark O'Connor and guitarist Ry Cooder, who coaxed a seductively languid, sleepwalking electric tone from his instruments. Albert Lee, a British musician, and my cousin David Lindley also joined us. Kenny Edwards, a former Stone Poneys bandmate, played an acoustic bass guitar made by Ferrington. "To Know Him Is to Love Him" was a number one country song for us, thanks to Emmy's angelic, soaring lead. Emmy also recommended Linda Thompson's bittersweet ballad "Telling Me Lies." It, too, became a hit single, and both songs received accolades.

Dolly, Emmy, and I had a lot of fun recording together, and we even squeezed a few television appearances and one later album into our three already overbooked schedules, but finding time to tour together was impossible, so we considered ourselves lucky to have had such a musically satisfying experience and let the rest go.

With musicians like the Beastie Boys and Bon Jovi dominating the charts in 1987, it was easy to see why record labels were scratching their brains, trying to figure out how to sell such a varied stew. Dolly had left her long standing label, RCA Records, so it was up to my firm, Elektra/Asylum, and Emmy's company, Warner Bros., to decide who would release it. I imagine the talks were more akin to a game of hot potato than a fierce fight for a desired product. It was eventually agreed that, because Warner had a country section, our record would be used to create an ad campaign aimed at the country music market.

To make matters worse, the corporate marketing gurus at the country music labels had chosen to begin utilising focus groups to test their products before they were made or launched. As an example, you could ask the focus group whether they preferred sad or happy tunes. "We like happy songs!" said the focus group, and the authors and producers were tasked with creating "happy" tunes to record. This was especially difficult for songwriters, who rarely feel the need to write when they are happy because they are too busy savouring the pleasure of happiness. When something awful happens, they try to find a way to go on, so they compose a song about it. Hank Williams, one of the finest and most successful country performers of all time, didn't write "happy" songs like "Your Cheatin' Heart" or "I'm So Lonesome I Could Cry," but they made the listener feel better. The listener received the impression that someone else had gone through an event comparable to the listener's own, and then went to the time and effort of precisely writing it down and sharing the experience, like a compassionate friend might. Hearing a song like "I'm So Lonesome I Could Cry" in this manner may make the listener feel better, or "happy." Our album, which included songs like the classic "Rosewood Casket," which conveyed the story of a dying and heartbroken sister's last wish, didn't fit the standards of the focus group.

Jim Ed Norman, the keyboard player in Shiloh, Don Henley's previous band before joining the Eagles, had recently been appointed head of Warner Bros. Records' country music division in Nashville. I assume he had the same disdain for the focus group approach to music promotion that we did. He sounded pleased that the project had fallen into his lap and worked hard to promote it. Trio debuted at number one on the country chart and remained there for five weeks. It debuted at number ten on the mainstream album chart and went on to win a Grammy and an Academy of Country Music Award. There were four country singles, including the number one "To Know Him Is to Love Him." It was certified platinum within a year.

The West Coast was pummelling by one fierce rainfall after another during the winter of 1979. The Pacific Coast Highway crumbled in a succession of dramatic mudslides, making driving home for weeks at a time impossible. I discovered that I could take a lengthy detour into Las Virgenes Canyon, but it was also prone to mudslides. This carried on for three months as the overwhelmed California Department of Transportation attempted to repair a road that should never have been built in the first place owing to intrinsic geological instability.

I was trapped in Malibu, watching the big waves wash the sand off the beach in front of my house, which had no foundation. The majority of the residences in Malibu Colony include a glass-enclosed space called a teahouse that extends from the main house out onto the beach. The waves were so high one night that they carried away the remainder of the sand from under my teahouse. It split away from the main house, my sofa cushions swirling in the surf like they were in a gigantic washing machine. I realised I had broken the desert's first rule: never buy a house near a flood plain.

I was with then-governor Jerry Brown when he came out to inspect the damage. By this point, the newspapers were speculating on whether the governor would use public funds to safeguard his girlfriend's home. Jerry had already decided not to, so I moved my furniture and things onto a moving van and shipped them to storage, knowing that my house would probably fall with the next crest of waves. Meanwhile, the rest of Malibu had heard that he wasn't going to pay money to safeguard the Colony since I lived there and felt they were being treated unfairly. They weren't his girlfriend, after all. I was expected to see mobs with pitchforks and torches demanding his hide. Jerry was trapped in a scenario he didn't create and for which he couldn't provide a permanent solution.

After Jerry spoke with residents all along the shore, the National Guard was sent in to sandbag, and the houses were spared. I decided to hunt for a house in town, away from the ever-present threat of the waves. I left Malibu certain that the California Coastal Commission was correct in insisting on no new construction on the beach because the residences are too susceptible, and development can alter the natural distribution of sand, culminating in exactly the situation I witnessed. I also feel that the beach should not be considered private property and that the general public should have free and unlimited access to it.

I discovered a lovely home on Rockingham Drive in Brentwood constructed by architect Paul Williams, whose work I had long loved. It had a blue slate roof, plenty of guest bedrooms, and a lovely garden for my two Akita dogs to run about in. Adam's songwriting career was taking off, so he relocated to Santa Monica. Nicolette finally moved in with me at the Rockingham house. So did our friend Danny Ferrington, a luthier from rural Louisiana who handcrafted magnificent guitars. He built them at the request of numerous musicians who approached him to make their fantasy guitars. To mention a few, they were Johnny Cash, Keith Richards, George Harrison, Eric Clapton, Richard Thompson, and Ry Cooder. He'd personalise them by incorporating design suggestions from the musicians, meeting both their visual and musical needs. The guitars always sounded fantastic, with the acoustics tailored to the individual's playing style, which he was intimately familiar with. His expertise rests in his ability to make the musician's most extravagant decorative fantasy appear tasteful. He constructed a miniature guitar for me to play while riding on our tour bus. It was made of rosewood, ebony, spruce, abalone, and mother-of-pearl and had a regular width neck and a tiny body to fit into tight areas. Even though I insisted on bunnies and tweeting birds in the design, the end product was exquisite. Each to their own.

CHAPTER 11

GETTING RESTLESS

My life had settled into a fairly normal pattern. I'd record an album every year, which would take a few months to finish, and the rest of the time we'd do one-night stands across the country. My records had sold so well by this point that instead of playing in tiny venues like the Troubadour, I was being booked into hockey stadiums and outdoor pavilions with large crowds. The sound in those massive spaces was similar to being in a flushing toilet with the lid down. I swear I could still hear the lead guitar solo from the band that had played the week before ricocheting off the walls and booming in the rafters. Those areas were filled with zombie sounds that refused to die, just becoming dimmer with time. People were wandering about, passing cigarettes, and drifting off in search of a hot dog or a cold beer at the concession stands that surrounded the upper decks.

Now, while I was thrilled and glad that the records were selling and that people were flocking to those dreadful-sounding arenas to hear me sing, I couldn't help but feel that both the spectators and the artists were getting a raw deal. The audience was hearing a sound mix that was so distorted by the building's acoustics that any delicate passages or musical nuances were lost. This had a sinister effect on how we composed music. We began to design our recordings, intentionally or unconsciously, to that gigantic arena sound because they couldn't hear anything but loud, high-arching guitar sections and a cavernous backbeat, and because they didn't want to hold still for anything they hadn't heard on one of the albums. This meant that any of the more delicate and well-crafted material, such as "Heart Like a Wheel" or "Hasten Down the Wind," had to be sandwiched between something that could withstand the onstage acoustics.

I clung to those tunes with tenacity, layering them into the recordings like pills in a hamburger. I knew that a melodious ballad would be a better fit for my voice. It would allow me to tap into a much richer emotional vein than what I used to refer to as a "short-note song." That is, an uptempo song written by a rock band to fit over a catchy riff, giving it something to do until the lead guitarist gets to play his Big Solo. This strategy resulted in some outstanding music from bands such as Cream and the Rolling Stones, but even those performers would frequently say that they missed the musical heat of their club days and wished they could play in more musically sympathetic surroundings. Those boomy venues blasted all the intricacies out of rock & roll as well, before playing midwife to the birth of heavy metal.

I was not surprised when the heavy metal band Metallica achieved a style that was huge and orchestral in its guitar textures, demonstrating itself to be perfectly capable of producing beautiful melodies with unusual, finely constructed harmonies. My twelve-year-old son was a committed metal shredder, and when I was watching him tear down a Metallica song and then reassemble it on the neck of his own guitar, I said that their stadium-sized guitar sounds reminded me of a symphony orchestra. He gave me a scathing teenage sneer. When Metallica released an album with the San Francisco Symphony conducted by Michael Tilson Thomas, I felt validated. All of this goes to show that musicians, like plants, seek out a rich acoustical environment, and I was no exception.

Another thing that made me upset about the change from clubs to arenas was that musicians didn't get to see each other play as much as they did when the folk rock music scene was centred on L.A.'s Troubadour or New York's Bitter End. The bathrooms were located in a back-hall area off the performance arena due to the Troubadour's restricted capacity. This meant that everyone from the bar had to walk through the room where the stage was to get to the plumbing. Even if you were an up-and-coming hopeful hanging around in the bar but couldn't afford the admittance charge, you could get a good taste of what was going on on stage whenever nature insisted. If you had previously been hired to play at the Troubadour by owner Doug Weston, you got free admission, so when someone interesting was playing, we veterans would swarm the staircase and the upstairs balcony night after night to see our favourites. I recall seeing Joni Mitchell, James Taylor, the Flying Burrito Brothers, George Carlin, and Steve Martin perform every night of a two-week engagement, two shows each night on weekdays and three on weekends. This allowed artists to perceive a broader range of another artist's abilities, resulting in some robust cross-pollination of musical styles.

Seeing each other's performances in stadiums did not come naturally. The tickets were much more expensive, excluding newcomers, there was no place to hang around and socialise socially, such as the Troubadour bar, unless one had rare and exclusive backstage access, and parking was a nightmare. Then there was the bad sound, which meant we couldn't listen to and analyse the music like we could in smaller settings. In short, the artists were less likely to trip over each other's influence and inspiration than they had been previously.

The incessant touring and endless repetition of the same songs over and over again created a creeping understanding that my music had grown to sound like my washing machine. In the late 1970s, a promotional trip that took us to the United Kingdom, Germany, and France startled us back into the forgotten reality of playing in smaller, devoted music venues. We were playing at medium-sized theatres with proscenium stages and lots of chubby-faced cherubs in bas-relief cavorting around the walls since I wasn't particularly well known in Europe. In addition to pleasing my Victorian sensibilities, the cherubs and other fussy design features softened the parallel surfaces of the theatre walls and sweetened the sound. Finally, the childhood fantasy of mine had come true: I was singing on a real stage in a real theatre with a curtain. I felt inspired.

The inspiration was fleeting. We were back in the States in no time, hitting the same old tour in the same distinctly boring arenas. Add to it the gnawing loneliness of a life spent constantly on the move, with insufficient time spent in any one place to foster relationships or build trust. I was starting to feel down. And imprisoned. We were playing in Atlanta one night. We'd spent the afternoon playing around in the few stores that had sprouted up in Underground Atlanta, the recently excavated, fire-charred ruins of the pre-Civil War metropolis. Big, smudgy, black-ringed eyes were popular at the time, and I discovered what appeared to be a particularly unusual way to accomplish them in one of the little stores. It was a new to me ancient cosmetic called kohl, which was some kind of black mineral powdered into a thin powder and had just arrived from India. There was also a blue one, which was unusual for me, but I reasoned that if I couldn't alter my life, I could at least change the colour of my eye makeup, so I purchased that as well. It came in a little clay pot with a pointed wooden stick fastened into the lid to serve as an applicator.

I was eager to try it out and went straight to the dressing room of the venue where we were playing (another arena) and began smearing the gunk around my eyes. I had mistakenly speckled my cheeks with what appeared to be blue measles because of my unfamiliarity with the applicator stick and powdered medium. I finished cleaning up all the stray blue blobs and wondered what I was going to do with the 45 minutes till I had to sing. I had completed the book I had in my bag and was scowling at the concrete floor, wishing we were still in a European theatre with cherubs and that I didn't have to face an all-night bus ride after the concert, when someone tapped on the door, waking me up. One of the security officers handed me a book that had been sent backstage with a note suggesting that it was something he or she thought I might enjoy. "Oh goody!" I said. "Now I won't have to be bored."

I took a glance at the cover: Colette's The Vagabond. "Never heard of this book," I remarked. I'd never heard of Colette before. She just had one name. Cher, for example. I opened the book and started reading. The story is set around 1910 in France. The Belle Epoque! My favourite epoch! Backstage in her dressing area, there is a woman my age who performs in music halls. She's drawing blue greasepaint circles around her eyes, and some of it has dripped down her cheek. Is it also blue for her? She also employs kohl. Kohl once again! I only found out about it that afternoon.

What else is there? She's a little bored. She has already finished the book she brought with her. She is getting ready to go onstage and perform her act. She has lost motivation to pursue her profession as "a woman of letters" and is now attempting to establish herself as "a woman on the stage." Things aren't going as smoothly as they could, and she realises she's "in for a bad fit of the blues." She is thinking about her puppy and her slightly awkward lover, whom she misses. There's a knock at her door... I have a devoted Akita dog and an awkward partner. I believe I'm "in for a bad case of the blues." I understand!

On the long bus ride home that night, I finished the book. I began to think about how I could operate in a more theatrical context, in smaller theatres, and not in a different location every night.

CHAPTER 12

MEETING JOE PAPP

I grabbed the nearest available phone and dialled John Rockwell in New York to complain about my situation. John has been writing about music for The New York Times for almost thirty years and is one of the few critics who can write authoritatively about both classical music and modern pop music. We first met in 1973, when he came to my Hollywood Hills residence on Beachwood Drive to interview me. He saw I had Otto Friedrich's Before the Deluge: A Portrait of Berlin in the 1920s on my shelf. (Yes, I did lend the book to Jackson Browne, who composed a terrific song with the same title. This is a common and legal practice. The title of Robert Heinlein's 1966 science-fiction masterpiece The Moon Is a Harsh Mistress came to mind. Jimmy Webb, the famous songwriter, loved the title and used it for a song on my CD Get Closer.) Before the Deluge was about the Weimar Republic in Germany, just as Hitler was gaining power, and all the squandered opportunities that could have prevented him from becoming dictator. I was fascinated by this era's tragedy, as well as the glamour of pre war Berlin, architectural innovation, the declining importance of virgin brides (no dowries in a bad economy), gender-bending clothing styles, hair and makeup styles, and wonderful music (Kurt Weill, the Comedian Harmonists). David Bowie was experimenting with one foreign picture after another, and his look in the mid-1970s felt disturbingly identical to that earlier time. I wondered if we were on the verge of our own Weimar Republic in the United States, to be followed by the harsh reality of fascism and aggressive imperialism.

Rockwell, who grew up in Germany, obtained his PhD in German cultural history, and published his thesis on the Weimar Republic, is a wealth of knowledge, and we became fast friends. When I phoned him to complain about my sluggish state of mind and the lack of angels in the architecture of my workplace, he advised that the next time I came to New York, he would take me to meet a man named Joe Papp. "Who exactly is Joe Papp?" I inquired. Joe Papp, intoned Rockwell, was a brilliant theatre man who had revolutionised Shakespeare interpretation by insisting on making it accessible across cultural, economic, and social lines, using racially diverse casts, and presenting it to the public for free at the Delacorte Theater in Central Park. He was also not reluctant to bring in performers from other fields. Perhaps he had some ideas about what to do with me.

When I returned to New York, Rockwell found a gap in his extremely busy schedule that corresponded to a gap in Joe Papp's even busier schedule and took me in a taxi to the New York Public Theater in Lower Manhattan. I was still unfamiliar with Papp and had no notion that he had aided in the birth of a staggering number of outstanding careers, including that of George C. Scott, Meryl Streep, James Earl Jones, Martin Sheen, and Wallace Shawn, as well as musicals like Hair and A Chorus Line.

Joe Papp was both clever and captivating. This is not something I say lightly. I could count the amount of men I've met who radiated his charisma and competence on one hand. There was also his attentive, inquisitive, and endlessly informed intelligence, which had the effect of a wild tiger on a frayed leash. He kindly listened to my manic rant about Colette and wanting to sing on a stage with a curtain, then went about his day meeting with individuals of incomparably greater ability and importance than me. I doubt he thought twice about our meeting.

Papp was enraged when the city cancelled his financing for staging Shakespeare in Central Park that summer, something he had done since 1962. He made the decision not to do Shakespeare that summer. He would instead perform Gilbert and Sullivan's operetta The Mikado. He approached famed director and author Wilford Leach about directing it, but Leach disliked Gilbert and Sullivan and stated he didn't think he wanted to do it. However, because Papp was so enthusiastic about the concept, Leach went to a record store to purchase a copy of The Mikado and instead returned home with a copy of The Pirates of Penzance. This he decided he liked, but the customary style of doing it was too rigid for him. Leach wanted to approach it as if it were a completely new play. He decided to use modern pop vocalists from our day because Gilbert and Sullivan was the pop music of the time.

When Leach woke up in the morning, he liked to watch the Today show. Coincidentally, John Rockwell had a monthly spot on the show discussing music. While Leach was casting Pirates, he overheard Rockwell discussing me on Today.

Leach liked my singing and believed that I was the right person to play Mabel, the soprano ingénue. When he walked into Papp's office to tell him about his idea, Papp said, "I've met her; she wants to work here." He directed his aide to contact me at my home in Malibu.

The call came in as I was upstairs showering. Jerry Brown was downstairs, next to the phone, so he picked it up. Jerry had seen H.M.S. Pinafore in school and recalled Gilbert and Sullivan from that, so when I walked downstairs, he informed me that someone named Joe Papp had called and asked me to sing in Pinafore. I was overjoyed! My sister had sung the alto role of Buttercup when I was six years old, and I had studied the soprano part of Josephine from the enormous Gilbert and Sullivan book that sat on our piano at home, and I loved her songs. I broke into a chorus of "Refrain Audacious Tar" before beginning to perform the small forlorn song "Sorry Her Lot." This was my favourite, and I didn't think I'd be able to sing it!

I instantly grabbed up the phone and dialled Joe Papp's number. I told him I'd love to perform Pinafore. When he stated it was Pirates, I was a little upset because I had never learnt those songs and wasn't sure if I would appreciate them as much. He informed me that Pirates had a plethora of great tunes for Mabel to sing, and that the part was mine if I wanted it. I then insisted on flying back to New York to audition for them, since I wanted to make sure that he and the director were pleased with the way I sang it. I didn't want any bad surprises.

I was worried about my appearance on the flight to New York. I was growing my hair out from the incredibly short cut I'd worn on the cover of my most recent album, Mad Love, and the back of my hair was streaked with big chunks of cyclamen pink. It was the early 1980s, and we were just getting started with the radically abnormal hair colours that I recall first seeing in their most foreboding splendour in Stanley Kubrick's A Clockwork Orange. I made the mistake of mixing the extreme colour process with a permanent to achieve Nicolette's curled hair, and my hair simply snapped off. The stringy parts that remained gave me the appearance of a Polish Crested chicken. I hacked them off with my sewing scissors, creating shambles that my usual hairdresser couldn't fix. Many of my actress friends told me that when they went to read for a part, they dressed up to look like the character they were trying to play. The Pirates of Penzance takes place in Victorian England. I liked vintage clothing and had some very exquisite white lace Victorian summer frocks in my wardrobe, but it was early spring and too chilly in New York for them, so I came into one of the Public Theater's rehearsal halls wearing cowboy boots, jeans, a sweater, and short pink hair. I didn't appear to be very Victorian. Joe Papp was there and introduced me to Wilford Leach and Bill Elliott, the music director. I liked them both right away, and that hasn't changed.

I had yet to see a Pirates score or hear a recording, which they said was unnecessary until they determined whether to perform the works in their original keys or move to other keys to accommodate the pop vocalists. I didn't like the concept of shifting keys because it can make the orchestra sound foggy at best, but I chose to keep quiet until we investigated it. We began at the piano, and I requested Bill to show me the highest notes recorded in the score for Mabel. He played a D above high C for me. I was singing the high C in my band's concerts night after night, so I didn't believe the D—one note higher on the scale—would be a problem. In the concert, I ended up singing Mabel's "Poor Wandering One" in two keys: the original and a lower key to add a more current feel. I had a really high voice with an upper extension that I never got to utilise much in rock and country except for a few flourishes and embellishments, so it wasn't as powerful as the range where I'd been belting "Heat Wave" and "Blue Bayou" for years. This was going to give me problems, but I didn't realise it yet. Also, like Violetta in La Traviata, Bill wrote me a cadenza (a short ornamental solo piece) to sing in the first act and again at the end of the show that went up to a very high E flat in the nosebleed octave. With eight shows every week, that would be sixteen E flats—something Violetta, who is feeble and consumptive, would never attempt in real opera. But I didn't realise it either. I went home and repacked my suitcase in preparation for a vacation to London. I'd been invited to perform on The Muppet Show and chose to bring my parents along for the experience, thinking they'd be able to explore the sites in London while I rehearsed with Kermit, Miss Piggy, and the rest of the vivacious Muppets group.

I had the Pirates score firmly packed between layers of pyjamas and the ancient Victorian garments I planned to wear on the show by this point. I'd also copied the vinyl disc recording to a cassette tape and put it in my new pink Sony Walkman, which was the hottest portable sound innovation at the time.

We slept at the Savoy Hotel, which is also adjacent to the Savoy Theatre, where the D'Oyly Carte actors played all of Gilbert and Sullivan's beloved operettas during Queen Victoria's reign. I've long admired this hotel's Victorian design, which was rebuilt in the 1930s in the Art Deco style. The suites we stayed in had high ceilings, beautiful mouldings, coal fireplaces, and buttons to call the room service waiter. He'd show up at any time of day or night, take the order, and return with a tea cart stocked with steaming pots of freshly brewed loose tea, dainty miniature tea sandwiches, and hot scones with jam and clotted cream. Yum! In case one had difficulties reaching the soap, there was also a button to summon the maid next to the sumptuously deep bathtub. I never used that button, but I did enjoy basking in the hot water, taking in all the historical elements of the curved doors, 1930s hardware, and freestanding sinks, all of which I replicated in a house I rebuilt in San Francisco years later. Our apartments had a beautiful view of the Thames, and the night following my first rehearsal with the Muppets, I got out the new score and put on my Walkman headphones. While listening to the lovely duet "Ah, Leave Me Not to Pine," I noticed Big Ben standing serenely in the moonlight. I was hearing the song for the first time in that location, where it had been created.

The original Muppet founders, Jim Henson and Frank Oz, were a lot of joy to work with. The first time I saw them perform was at the 1979 Grammy Awards. I arrived while the Muppets were still rehearsing, so I could witness the contortionist stances that Henson and Oz had to assume in order to get the puppets to move appropriately for the cameras. They could see how the puppets appeared from the camera's perspective by viewing small video monitors. I was completely captivated and impressed by their creativity, and I've been a devoted follower of puppetry ever since.

I was thrilled to be working with them and fantasised about having a romance with Kermit. I proposed a song, the Gershwins' "I've Got a Crush on You," to sing to him in a confessional tone, and then a rock-and-roll tune, "The Shoop Shoop Song (It's in His Kiss)," to sing after he kissed me. (I was warned that if my lipstick touched his green felt lips, it would stain and the Creature Shop would have to build a new body.) Our affair was doomed because Kermit had already made a serious commitment to Miss Piggy, and we had to part like Humphrey Bogart and Ingrid Bergman in the final scene of Casablanca. The entire Muppets cast, including a surprisingly forgiving Piggy, joined Kermit and me in a finale of "When I Grow Too Old to Dream," a 1930s standard I'd recorded on my CD Living in the USA. I sang "Blue Bayou" in the aforementioned Victorian togs and bare feet somewhere in the middle, accompanied by a chorus of frogs singing from lily pads floating in an artificial bayou. The set was designed to look like the Blue Bayou restaurant in Disneyland's Pirates of the Caribbean attraction. It was insanely entertaining.

I often wonder what a scientist like Oliver Sacks would learn about how the human brain compartmentalised if he had observed our rehearsals. During pauses, the puppeteers would sit and chat, speaking as themselves and also completely chiming in as the one or more puppet characters they had just operated. The puppets would occasionally squabble among themselves, or Miss Piggy would make scathing remarks about the script to her operator, Frank Oz, as he was composing it. The result was a lovely and brilliantly creative chaos, with people casually walking into and out of reality for hours at a time while being paid to do so.

Years later, Kermit and I rejoined briefly (much too briefly, in my opinion) to sing a duet of "All I Have to Do Is Dream" on a Muppets album. He went back to his love nest with that pig, and I never saw him again.

CHAPTER 13

THE PIRATES OF PENZANCE

I returned from my Muppet Show experience to the new house I had purchased in Rockingham, which had almost no furnishings, and began preparing to relocate to New York for the summer. I'd discovered an apartment on Manhattan's Upper West Side and was curious about life in New York City's really urban, tightly packed, and tremendously fascinating atmosphere.

My manager, Peter Asher, felt it was a brilliant idea for me to do Pirates, though he was rightly concerned that it would disturb the safe pattern of an album and many tours a year, and could harm the momentum he'd been able to build into my career.

He tried his best, based on his own theatre expertise, to give me a crash course in theatre etiquette and protocol so that I wouldn't upset the others from plain ignorance. I learned that the most essential thing was to never be late. Being late is a huge burden on the cast and crew, who don't like twiddling their thumbs while waiting for a self-absorbed, unprofessional rock star, and can run up the expense in an already stretched budget. It is certain to incite resentment.

The first day of practice, I made sure to leave with enough time to catch a cab and make it all the way from West 71st Street to the Public Theater in Greenwich Village. How long would it take to cover the entire island? However, the cabbie understood that his customer in the backseat was unfamiliar with the city, so he took an extra-long route. When I eventually arrived, I was fifteen or twenty minutes late and completely ashamed. It earned me a severe reprimand from our stage manager and was never repeated.

Just before meeting Rex Smith, who had been cast to portray Frederic opposite me, I was shown a life-size cutout portrait of Rex dressed in nothing more than his tremendous male pulchritude. It had somehow appeared near the practice room's door. Rex was probably writhing, but he didn't crack. He was so attractive that I was moaning inside, hoping he wasn't full of a glamour-boy attitude. He didn't. He was energetic and eager, a touch naive, quite candid, and had excellent instincts. I made the decision to like him.

A rehearsal room is a dangerous place. It usually consists of only the necessary number of chairs and the talent that people bring with them. The task will feel effortless if their talents are compatible and synergistic, and a clear notion emerges. It has the potential to become joyful with luck.

No matter how well chosen the actors or musicians, or how great the writer or director, the whole can become less than the sum of its parts. The work becomes morbidly difficult at this point. Anguish descends like a leaden slime, and the players are eager to be done and out of that place. It's difficult to stress how humiliating and unpleasant this feels, even when no one is to blame. Although I am not religious, a rehearsal room can appear to be a sacred environment; a place for transformation. A performer enters at his own risk. Rex was aware of this. He grasped my hand as we walked into Joe Papp's Public Theater's rehearsal room, his eyes wide with expectation and joy. "It's like going to church," he explained.

After introducing ourselves and the characters we were portraying, the first thing we did at rehearsal was sit down and sing the entire show from beginning to end. This was exciting since there are numerous prominent choral parts, and we got to hear how the vocal ensemble would work with its more natural approach to singing the Victorian melodies. Wilford and Bill decided to add another song for me to sing and asked if I could recommend something from another Gilbert and Sullivan production. I think I could! "'Sorry Her Lot'!" I screamed. "It's a Pinafore!" "I already know!" I performed it for them. It was ideal for the location they had in mind. I was overjoyed to be able to perform the song I had loved since childhood. I couldn't wait to tell my sister about it.

The next days found us on our feet and "off book," with a chance to witness what choreographer Graciela Daniele had prepared. Tony Azito, who played the constable, got up and did a fantastic rubber-jointed dance to complement his lament about being a cop. His reedy voice echoed Berlin cabaret while somehow retaining the asceticism of monastery chant. I was out of breath.

Kevin Kline began to perform some fantastic physical antics to make his character appear handsome, bold, and hopelessly bewildered all at once: Errol Flynn with a touch of dementia. I can see snippets of Kevin's Pirate King piled into Johnny Depp's Captain Jack Sparrow, the character he created for the film Pirates of the Caribbean.

Rex was clearly enslaved to Kevin, so his persona followed the Pirate King around the stage like a puppy dog. This created a beautiful relationship between the two male heartthrobs, and they never had to compete.

George Rose was our Major-General Stanley. He humbled us all with his lightning-fast patter songs, despite being a seasoned theatrical professional to the tenth power. These had been prepared to a level of perfection that I would not have thought possible before rehearsals even began. He was stunning.

Patricia Routledge, another brilliant product of British musical theatre, sung and portrayed Nurse Ruth's wacky Victorian tunes and demeanour with tremendous naturalness and seamless comedic brilliance. I overheard her remark something to Kevin while they were rehearsing a scene one day, she being the seasoned pro and he the new rising star. "Kevin, what do you think we're trying to accomplish with this scene?" she said. Kevin responded, "To make it funny?"

"No," she said, quite sternly. "There's no need to make it amusing. We must make it obvious. It will be funny if it is apparent." Kevin and I both thought this was excellent advice. I try to incorporate it into everything I sing. For example, if one is singing a sorrowful song, it is preferable to express the story as clearly and simply as possible—even journalistically. It will have a greater impact on the audience and appear more emotional than a teary, overblown performance.

Finally, Mabel's joyful sisters' female chorus emerged as an amalgamated star in their own right. On a nightly basis, they emitted wonderful comedic parts and vocals that tracked a bipolar flip from angelic beauty to brassy belting.

With a cast this polished and appealing, I imagined the play would move like a locomotive, and I'd be carried along by sheer momentum as long as I didn't fall down on stage. I hadn't realised I was acting because my words were all sung, and my performance still required some fleshing out in order for Mabel's persona to emerge.

Wilford was the type of director who let his performers do their work, but I knew nothing about acting and was feeling lost. We were rehearsing outside in the hot sun at the Delacorte Theater in Central Park, which was about to open. The combination of that summer's record-breaking temperaturesBreaking temperatures and oppressive humidity made me long for the relative comfort of Arizona's dry heat. Keith David, a Juilliard trained actor with one of the greatest pirate voices, asked me what was on Mabel's mind. "A sno-cone!" says one. I reacted frantically. Keith was considerate. "Mabel wants Frederic," he stated to me. Her environment is devoid of heat. Frederic is the only one." Molly, my large black Akita dog, was panting in the shadow at the side of the stage. Molly and I had been in the park for nearly a week, and she had grown particularly fond of the squirrels. She developed an incredible concentration when she saw one, which permeated and moulded her entire body. She pricked her ears, tilted her head, and gave her entire fluffy self over to one impulse. That's what I decided to do. Mabel was born after I transformed myself into a canine soprano. I knew I was there when Robin Boudreau, one of the girls in the chorus, mentioned one day that pets and their owners often resembled each other. Mabel was likewise pigeon-toed, although I am duck-footed. Mabel's cooler side must have been concerned by the desperate, rushing motion towards Frederic's direction, for her feet kept trying to turn around and flee away. In what I suppose was the most fundamental beginnings of the craft of acting, a weird little collection of idiosyncrasies and urges like these began to sprout and bloom in me. Rudimentary was the best I ever got, but it was enough to keep me going around the stage for the entire year I was with the program. Pirates first aired on July 15, 1980. My birthday had arrived.

People frequently characterise the Public Theater's summer shows in Central Park as enchanting, and while this may sound like an overused phrase, it is quite correct. Shape shifting and transcending mundane conditions are frequently associated with the concept of magic, and that is exactly what you get with superb theatre. There was also the element of time travel for me. Night after night, I stood by the side of the stage in my Victorian bonnet and white summer gown, a gentle breeze ruffling my skirt and the moon gliding softly overhead. A huge pond beyond me provided a nice natural extension to our painted sea. A meteorological station was placed in Belvedere Castle, a Gothic-style observation tower built in 1867, on the opposite shore. Just beyond the tree line was a still-standing Art Deco silhouette of the 1930s Manhattan cityscape. It felt like Fred Astaire himself could have sprung out of that skyline, top hat and cane in hand, and tap-danced on the moon. Living in such a densely populated area, the opportunities to enjoy nature's nocturnal wonders are primarily confined to ball games and trips to Coney Island beach. A baseball fan may disagree, but I believe both experiences pale in comparison to an evening in Joe Papp's magic theatre in the wide outdoors of Central Park.

It has some disadvantages. We were terrified by lightning, battered by wind, and soaked by rain, which turned our outfits into Saran Wrap. There were also bugs. We swallowed them every night while singing, but once, just before the kissing moment I had with Rex at the conclusion of the second act, an enormous mosquito got stuck in the gluey coating of my lip gloss. It was straining to break free, and when Rex leaned in to kiss me, his eyes bulged out of his head. He, like me, was battling to retain his cool. Rex got to leave the stage after our kiss, but I had to stay and sing "Sorry Her Lot" from start to finish while a gigantic insect played its death scene on my lower lip.

Papp arrived at my dressing room door one night, accompanied by Mayor Ed Koch. In retrospect, I believe Joe brought him down to watch our highly popular performance and meet the performers in an attempt to recoup his financing. I wasn't aware of any of these political subplots at the time, but I knew the photographer he had with him: a particularly aggressive paparazzo stationed himself at the park's Eighty-Second Street entrance. There were no automobiles allowed in that area, so I was on foot and at his mercy every day as he swooped and dived at me, calling me the b-word, the c-word—any filthy thing he could think of to elicit an emotional response and end up with a more fascinating photo to sell. Richard, my bodyguard, would tell me from the corner of his lips that his job was to keep me from hitting the photographer with a rock since it would very certainly result in a lawsuit. I was polite.

But when I saw the photographer's smugly pleased grin as he stood behind Papp and Mayor Koch taking shots of me in my bathrobe and pin curls, my face splashed with cold cream, I didn't behave. I don't have an especially short temper because my personality is slightly phlegmatic. In reality, I have a really long fuse. The only problem is that when it finally catches fire, it is linked to an ice-covered volcano. The icy part of me was calmly and logically explaining to Joe that the fellow had been tormenting me for a couple of weeks, that I didn't think it was fair, and that I was going to strangle him with his camera strap and then smash the hated camera on the concrete floor, causing the film to roll out and rendering the photos useless. I suppose I was successful because the photos never appeared. I then strolled calmly to the showers at the end of the hall to wash away the remaining makeup and cold cream, as well as the sticky heat of the July night. When I returned, Joe was still standing in the corridor with the rather surprised mayor, emphasising how crucial temperament was for actresses.

Because of our unexpected success in Central Park, Joe Papp began making plans to relocate Pirates to Broadway in the fall. Even though it meant leaving behind my barely-moved-into new house, friends, and love commitments, this looked like a fantastic plan to me. Peter Asher, a more realistic thinker than I, warned me that it would also disrupt the lucrative album-tour, album-tour routine that we had gotten into so comfortably over the previous four years.

Another issue was that Peter and Joe Papp did not click from the moment they laid eyes on each other. This scenario gradually improved because both were men of their word and diligent experts, although it was awkward at first. Joe's inner street fighter was brought out by Peter's polished demeanour. I urged Peter to let me negotiate with Papp on my own for the first round, and then he could complete the deal. Of course, this was a ridiculous idea, because artists cannot effectively advocate for themselves. I told Peter that all I wanted to do was get the show to Broadway and not get rich doing it. In response, he grumbled that he didn't want me to become destitute, then threw up his hands and let me have my way.

Joe came to my apartment a few days later to discuss the transfer to Broadway. He took a cigar and a couple of Spike Jones CDs with him. Rex and I had been there for a couple of hours, blasting Mick Jagger's rendition of "Beast of Burden" from the Rolling Stones' Some Girls album. Joe immediately enforced order by turning on Spike Jones, the American screwball comedy bandleader of the 1940s and 1950s, and we spent the next hour howling on the floor. Rex was also an admirer of Spike Jones. Joe then slammed us with puns for another half hour. He was devilishly excellent at it. It was then time to get down to business, so Rex walked home and Joe lit the cigar.

I informed Joe that I was in the process of purchasing an apartment so that I would have a place of my own when we moved to Broadway. The actress Liv Ullmann lived at the apartment. Ullmann had recently sung and danced for Joe Papp in a production of I Remember Mama, and had resided in the flat while doing so, in addition to acting in my favourite Ingmar Bergman films. I assumed she was making enough money to cover her expenditures there. Also, while Liv Ullmann wasn't a household name on Broadway, she was a huge success in another industry, so I felt our two situations were comparable. I won't even bother pointing out how absurd this thinking was. Joe must have been laughing inside at my folly. I want the same compensation as Ullmann. Of course, I had no idea what she got, and I still don't. Joe ended up making a great offer that included certain bonuses I never would have thought to ask for in the first place, much to Peter's and my surprise. Perhaps he was taken aback by my lack of hostility and didn't want to be perceived as anything less than a gentleman when conducting business on such an uneven playing field. Anyway, we struck a bargain. The transition to Broadway went relatively smoothly. Patricia Routledge was unavailable for the Broadway run, therefore the cast was changed. Estelle Parsons, a veteran actor, took her place and garnered rave reviews for her portrayal as Ruth, the zany nursery maid. The show began previews in the fall, and we formally opened on January 8, 1981, at the Uris Theatre on West Fifty-First Street.

During previews, we were practising one version of the show in the afternoon and presenting another in the evening. This was exhausting because we did eight shows a week, plus rehearsals, for a total of sixteen. They added performances on the Today program and Saturday Night Live to their rehearsal schedule. This meant getting up at four a.m. for the Today show and staying up until four a.m. to perform on Saturday Night Live. We had a matinée performance on Christmas Day and were absolutely exhausted by New Year's Eve. We'd already done a matinée that afternoon, and the pit band had gone out and gotten quite drunk in between gigs. (Can you blame them?) Rex and I were staggering around the stage with shredded vocal cords, uncomfortably sober. The orchestra pit emitted strange, unknown sounds. The trumpet player who played the lead into Rex's and my emotional duet at the end of act one was either a lot more intoxicated or more nakedly exposed than the rest. He sounded dreadful. And raucous. Giggling is a nervous system affliction that I believe is encoded into some people's physiology and appears to be a reaction to extreme nerves, exhaustion, or self-consciousness. It's rarely a pleasant experience for the giggler, and it can seem like trying to cross Niagara Falls without a barrel. Rex and I couldn't stop laughing at the horrible trumpet blasts and couldn't stop ourselves. Breaking character onstage is the biggest sin an actor can make. This breaks the audience's enchantment, making it nearly impossible to win them back. Our audience, who had paid good money for tickets to attend our now hopelessly amateur show, was not amused. They started booing. Rex and I, still reeling from our nervous system's tantrums and meltdowns, finished our songs as best we could and exited the stage.

Rex's eyes were wide with dread and true pain backstage. I was mortified and wringing my hands. Wilford Leach was concerned and, to his credit, did not yell at us, even though he would have been right in doing so. He instructed me to change into my second act outfit and, with Rex by my side, go out onto the stage before the play resumed and apologise to the crowd. It was the correct thing to do, but it felt like I was facing a firing squad. I'm not sure what I said to the audience, but that cleared the way for the second act to begin, and we concluded the concert without incident.

I had never received any formal voice instruction before starting at Pirates. The show's vocal demands were high, so a fantastic voice coach known as "Magic Marge," Marge Rivingston, was brought in to work with the entire cast. She was our mother hen, therapist, and taskmaster, and she always seemed to have the right piece of advice, whether personal or professional, to get us through the show. Bill Elliott had the girls' chorus belting out high notes that were originally meant to be performed in the upper extension of the voice—the range of an operatic soprano. That sounded funnier, and more like the contemporary pop style Wilford Leach had in mind for the performance. Without Marge's cautious direction, eight weeks of belting high notes may have caused major voice difficulties for the choir.

My issue was the inverse. I had an overdeveloped belt range and an underdeveloped upper extension as a result of all those years of screaming over a rock band. My high voice sounded more like a choir boy's than a grown-up lady opera singer's because my boy soprano brother Peter was my first inspiration. Rex and I had developed the bad habit of muscling our way through difficult vocal territory and, for lack of a better word, yelling. Marge set to work solving these issues. The largest challenge we had was that the Broadway schedule only allowed for one day of relaxation per week, which is insufficient for vocal rehabilitation. While performing the show, I was attempting to learn a healthy singing method, and the new muscles were attempting to gain strength despite not having enough time to rest. My voice eventually gave up, and I had to miss five gigs. This is something that every Broadway performer strives to avoid. There are several reasons for this, including the fact that the performance loses money from ticket cancellations if the star does not appear, the dynamic between the performers changes dramatically when a new person arrives, and the feeling that the missing cast member has let down the entire production. I was back on stage as soon as I could squeak. Marge's teaching helped my voice build enough strength to get me through the tough program. I never missed another performance after that.

CHAPTER 14

JERRY WEXLER AND THE GREAT AMERICAN SONGBOOK

I like working at Pirates and the fact that I didn't have to travel to a new location every night, but by early spring 1981, I was ready to try some new music. I felt I needed to focus on my phrasing—the aspect of my musicianship that I had always considered to be my weakest— in order to be a greater singer when I eventually returned to pop music. My customary approach to musical improvement was to study what came before whatever I was interested in better. Pop vocalists that came before me were interpreters of American standards. I began to recall the albums my father had brought home to play on the large high-fidelity monaural record player he had purchased in 1957: Ella Fitzgerald and Louis Armstrong duets, Peggy Lee, Chris Connor, June Christy, and Billie Holiday.

When in New York, I became acquainted with Jerry Wexler and his wife, Renee, whom I had met briefly when working for David Geffen and Elliot Roberts. Wexler was a well-known A&R executive in the music industry. He began his career as a reporter for Billboard magazine in the 1940s, where he created the term "rhythm and blues" to replace the distasteful "race records." Then, in 1953, he formed a partnership with Ahmet Ertegun and his brother, Nesuhi, and they co-founded the Atlantic record company, signing cultural icons such as Ray Charles, Aretha Franklin, Chris Connor, Dusty Springfield, Wilson Pickett, and Led Zeppelin. Needless to say, he possessed an impressive record collection. I suggested to him one evening that I intended to spend some time studying the singers who ruled before rock & roll transformed everything, and he provided me access to his vinyl bank.

Wexler had a quirky appeal that he tempered with hipster street idioms and perspective views, in addition to a tremendous career. He spoke like a Jewish bebopper with a Jesuit education at the age of sixty-four. His ears protrude slightly, as if he were on alert, giving the impression that he was paying close attention. Wexler voiced his enthusiastic approbation by describing Hamill as his favourite type of fellow: "an educated cat from a bad neighbourhood." I enjoyed hearing Wexler's stories about the musicians, songwriters, bullies, and hangers-on he met throughout his long tenure at the centre of the business. He was an excellent tutor.

Hamill, too, had an impressive record collection, primarily of jazz. He introduced me to tenor saxophonist Lester Young and trumpeter Clifford Brown, both of whom I admired for their lyrical playing styles. He had exquisite taste, and when he was writing, he was constantly listening to something enticing on his turntable. In addition to jazz, he would occasionally perform tunes by the legendary Mexican composer Cuco Sanchez. Years later, I used several of them on my Mexican records. He handed me a female rendition of "What's New," which was somewhat more in tune with my key than Sinatra's, and a magnificent recording of Betty Carter singing "Tell Him I Said Hello," which I recorded in 2004, with John Boylan and George Massenburg producing. Hamill's contribution was critical. Wexler and I were browsing through the recordings of Mildred Bailey, a jazz vocalist from the 1930s, when it occurred to me that I should make a concerted attempt to study the songs. I decided to form a practice band so that I could truly work on the phrasing. Wexler offered to assist me. We were producing a record before I realised it.

We began on an experimental basis, working in the afternoons before I had to go to the theatre to perform Pirates. Wexler assembled a great band of seasoned jazz musicians, many of whom had previously played with the genre's original interpreters. They included guitarist Tal Farlow, trumpeter Ira Sullivan, and pianist Tommy Flanagan, among others. I expected us to go into the studio and rehearse and build the arrangements as we went. Wexler had different plans and hired saxophonist Al Cohn to create the charts. Unfortunately, Al, who was a fantastic arranger, hadn't gotten any feedback from me before he prepared the charts, so I stumbled over some of the songs that were arranged at a quick tempo while I had pictured them sluggish and sombre. Parts of songs that I would have wanted to sing rubato were tightly tied to the rhythm section. "Never Will I Marry," a song I'd longed to perform for years, moved at such a fast rate that I couldn't swallow or breathe, let alone words. Wexler thought it was fine. I started to worry that we weren't a good fit in the studio and that I'd jumped in too fast. He had the unpleasant habit of leaning on the talk-back mike and interrupting me in the middle of a song to offer feedback on my rendition. I believed the interpretation to be my sole domain, therefore I was irritated as well.

I finished my run in Pirates and headed back to the West Coast. Wexler flew out with our master recordings, and we played the rough mixes for Joe Smith, another renowned record man who was also the president of my label at the time. Smith and Peter Asher believed the project was a mistake from the start and did not believe the music should be released. I agreed with them on the tracks, but I still wanted to record them because I liked them. Wexler thought the recording was fantastic and strongly advocated for its release. He wanted to finish mixing it, and we decided to let him since we respected his position in the industry, even though I knew it wouldn't alter our ultimate decision.

What convinced me that our disagreements were irreconcilable was learning that he intended to leave the mixing procedure fully up to the engineer, with neither of us there. The mixing process, which may drastically alter the sound and emotional impact of a recording, is far too critical to entrust to someone else. A bad recording cannot be saved, while a good one can be destroyed. Working with Peter, not only did I have a lot of say in the arrangements, but he and I also mixed the records with our engineer. Wexler was dismissive of this, telling me that he frequently listened to the mixes over the phone and provided his last thoughts. He advised that I listen to them over the phone and make any recommendations that sprang to mind. I was taken aback. The telephone cannot even begin to transmit the entire range of sound. String and a paper cup would suffice. I concluded he either didn't know the difference or assumed I didn't know the difference. Either option was unacceptable.

I discovered why Wexler acted the way he did after speaking with some musician friends who had worked on some of his previous productions. Wexler was a traditional A&R man in every way. In the early days of record production, the A&R guy may choose the material and musical arrangement for an artist like Rosemary Clooney. He would tell her, "I have this song called 'Come On-a My House.'" We'll record it in this style, with this arranger and these musicians." Rosemary, a brilliant vocalist with, I'm sure, lots of her own thoughts, had little to say about it. Bob Dylan and the Beatles changed everything. They created or chose their own material and musical direction, and were extremely successful as a result. Asylum, David Geffen's record company, was created on the idea that the artist's vision would be acknowledged and supported.

Wexler was a fantastic Monday morning quarterback in every sense of the term. He could tell when something was good after it happened. He could develop and coordinate broad musical directions, but musical specifics and engineering decisions were delegated to specialists on whom he relied significantly. Perhaps a lot more than he realised.

In my situation, hindsight reveals that his A&R instincts were correct in believing that I might be successful in recording standards from the American songbook, but he couldn't execute the recording in a way that satisfied me or my record label. I had to break the news to him that the record would not be released. I felt bad because he was upset and angry. I was devastated that the idea had failed, and much more devastated that I had lost his relationship. He and Renee had been quite nice to me while I was living in New York, and I really liked them both. There was no way to save the relationship under the circumstances.

While Peter Asher and Joe Smith were concerned about the money lost on the record, they were glad that it was not being released, which would have required them to throw good money after bad.

They hoped I'd forget about recording American classic songbook selections. No, I didn't.

Rex Smith, Kevin Kline, Tony Azito, George Rose, and I were requested to continue our roles in the film project after Joe Papp and Wilford Leach chose to make The Pirates of Penzance into a motion picture. We planned to shoot in London, so the rest of the ensemble, including Angela Lansbury, would be British.

Throughout the winter, we shot at Shepperton Studios in Surrey, roughly 45 minutes outside of London. Because the days were so short, our timetable placed us in the studio soon before the sun rose and out immediately after it set. I rented a room with a coal stove at the lovely old Connaught Hotel and attempted to stay warm by washing my clothing in the bathtub on rare days off.

Pete Hamill came and remained for a while, bringing me a steady stream of books he bought from a Charing Cross bookstore. I read them while waiting to be called on set: Henry James, Edith Wharton, Thomas Hardy, Flaubert, Turgenev, and Zola. They gave the clownish Victorian operetta I was singing a richer and more intellectual backdrop. It also inspired me to quote Flaubert: "Be regular and orderly in your everyday life, like a bourgeois, so you can be violent and original in your work." I've never fully matched either end of this equation, but it's a goal to strive for.

My father called one day and told me, in a tight, colourless voice, that my mother, who had been ill for a while, had died. When I was washing my clothes in the bathtub the next day off, I remembered when I was three, following my mother down the tiny walk to the clothesline and handing her clothespins while she hung out the family laundry. It always included my Raggedy Ann doll's blue calico frock and small white pinafore.

As spring approached, I ventured out one morning in the dark for my normal long drive. I was listening to a cassette of my old favourite Sinatra album, Only the Lonely, while missing my mother and still feeling disappointed over my missed opportunity to perform the beautiful songs I had picked for the ill-fated Wexler record. Just as Sinatra began his faultless delivery of "Guess I'll Hang My Tears Out to Dry," the sun appeared over the horizon, sticking to its new spring schedule. The sunlight and music filled me with longing and joy as a desert dweller stranded in the cold, dark North. I instantly realised that if I didn't capture the music I loved, I'd spend the rest of my life feeling like I'd lost out on an important experience. I resolved to beg Peter for assistance, and he agreed against his better judgement.

In his practical hat, Peter persuaded me that we should first produce an album of the more current music that my audience had grown to anticipate from me. I promptly started gathering material for a new album, Get Closer. Because our regular engineer, Val Garay, was unavailable, I proposed to Peter that we try George Massenburg, with whom I had previously recorded in Maryland. Peter had never worked with George before, but he admired the Complex, George's new studio in West Los Angeles.

In the business, George was considered as one of the great forefathers of computer-assisted mixing, as well as the developer of contemporary equalisation, which he invented as a teenager in his Baltimore garage. He had a puzzled expression on his face, similar to the glassy-eyed stare of a stuffed animal. He didn't dress like a rock star, instead opting for a regular boy's hairstyle, crewneck sweaters, and chinos. George, who was both handsome and uncomfortable, self-effacing and bashful, was able to perform multiple processes in his brain at the same time, ranging from a volcanic degree of invention to a cosmic slumber. I felt like I was sitting next to an unmanaged steam boiler that was overheating and perilously near to exploding while working with him day after day in front of the massive recording console he had created. The mood in his studio reminded me of the Japanese animation classic Howl's Moving Castle, with each track on the console acting as a portal into its own realm. What I learned from him completely altered my attitude to singing, recording, and listening.

I made my first digital album, Mad Love, in 1980. Because digital recording was a new technology then, Peter and I had not fully explored the broad range of possibilities that it offered. For instance, with analog recording, we had never developed a very sophisticated way to improve my vocal performances. As a result, most of my vocal tracks up until then had stayed exactly as I had sung them while we were recording the basic track. As we often worked on one song for hours, I would have to hold back to save my voice. Also, I was less inclined to take chances, because I was afraid I would be stuck with an idea that hadn't turned out right. The new technology greatly enhanced the ability to switch among many takes of different vocal approaches and edit together the best bits. We could drop in the most microscopic segments: a breath, a final consonant, a syllable that had wavered out of tune. A brilliant engineer like George, with his ability to hear sound in tremendous detail, knew how to match the pieces so that the edits were invisible and the singing sounded completely natural. This freed me to relax and sing anything that I wanted without having to worry that I would be stuck with something I didn't like. It also gave me a way to study the way my voice interfaced with the instrumental track, and I learned to phrase better and refine and develop new vocal textures. In short, what George had presented to me was a way to learn how to sing. We continued to work together for many years, and the learning never stopped. Peter worked beautifully with George, and the three of us became a comfortable team.

CHAPTER 15

NELSON RIDDLE

"Today Nelson Riddle is coming to my house, and I am going to sing Irving Berlin's beautiful song 'What'll I Do?' ' I woke up in the bedroom of my house on Rockingham Drive wondering. My face lit up with a wide grin. I went deeper into the covers, running through the tune in my head: "What'll I do? / When you're far... away...?" The song's beauty was shown in simple poetry and three-quarter time.

I got out of bed and ran to the bathroom to take a bath and dress. I'd been looking forward to this for a long time. I didn't want to be the source of any further delays.

I had decided that instead of a horn band, I would record my standards with an orchestra. I'd told Pete Hamill that I wanted the orchestrations to sound like Nelson Riddle, but that I didn't know any arrangers who could compose like him. "Why don't you just call Nelson Riddle?" he reasoned. I had not considered the possibility. There were various causes behind this:

a. I didn't know if he was still alive. (Easy enough to check.)

b. I didn't know if he knew I was alive, or cared.

c. I imagined that he didn't like music with rock underpinnings and would not be interested in working with a singer from that genre.

Nelson, who was sixty at the time, didn't know who I was when Peter Asher contacted him. He asked Rosemary, his daughter, if she thought he should work with me. "Well, Dad, the check won't bounce," she responded. She asked him to think about it. Nelson's phone hadn't been ringing much in recent years, despite the fact that he had created arrangements for some of popular music's greatest performers, including Nat "King" Cole, Ella Fitzgerald, Peggy Lee, Rosemary Clooney, and, of course, Sinatra. Most of his jobs had been lost to the rock-and-roll revolution, and he had been surviving by writing TV music and the occasional film soundtrack.

He met us at the Complex, where Peter, George, and I were finishing up the Get Closer mixes. I expressed my admiration for his work on Sinatra's Only the Lonely and how much it had meant to me over the years. We played him our version of "The Moon Is a Harsh Mistress," one of Get Closer's tunes. I informed him that my mother had recently died, and the song reminded me of her because I had always seen her face on the moon when I was a little child. He explained that his mother died when he was working on Only the Lonely, and that there was a lot of her in the arrangements. I timidly asked him if he would consider arranging a couple pieces for my upcoming standards album. To ask for more sounded arrogant. Nelson said that the Beatles had requested him to compose an orchestral arrangement for a song on one of their albums. He had flatly refused, stating that he only performed albums and not tracks. I took out the list of music I'd chosen. "Could you do all of these?" I inquired. He stated that he could.

We dashed to the piano. The opening track on the playlist was "Guess I'll Hang My Tears Out to Dry." Nelson reached into his briefcase and pulled out the original sketch of Sinatra's arrangement. Naturally, it would not be the correct key. We tried a few different things before we discovered one that worked for me. He crossed out Sinatra's key and replaced it with mine. Our work had started. Nelson took the sketch home and began working on a new arrangement in the new key. The incident stunned me.

I told Nelson that I wanted a really customised fit for my arrangements and that I wanted to be involved from the start. He liked the idea. We worked at the piano for a few hours the morning he arrived at my house, lugging the big briefcase. We largely chose keys and tempos. I provided him general directions but left the musical complexities of the orchestrations to him. More was way beyond my abilities. Sometimes I proposed that if I desired a rubato sensation with simple strings and woodwinds, I would bring in the rhythm section. While we were practising "Guess I'll Hang My Tears Out to Dry," I requested a key change to a higher key to raise the arrangement. Nelson shocked me by demonstrating how to modulate to a lower key, resulting in an elegant shift in mood.

After we finished rehearsing, we sat on the sofa and spoke about our lives. I told him about an unrequited infatuation I had on a composer we both knew, and he told me about his deep love for singer Rosemary Clooney, as well as the torch he had carried for many years. He told me about Irving Berlin proposing to his girlfriend and her father forbidding marriage, shattering his heart and driving him to write "What'll I Do?" They eventually married. We became good buddies.

Joe Smith came to my house before we started recording What's New to make one more attempt to talk me out of it. He was truly anxious that my audience would be offended and that my career would never recover. He thought I was squandering my professional life with both hands. He was correct by all reasonable means of assessing the circumstance. Joe Smith was a fantastic record producer. He was someone I admired, respected, and trusted. Normally, I would have paid attention to him. Fortunately, I had the Gershwins', Rodgers and Hart's, and Irving Berlin's tunes playing in my head, so I couldn't hear a word he said.

He realised his argument was having no effect on me. "I have Nelson Riddle on board, you know," I told him. He's consented to compose my arrangements." Smith simply sighed and asked if he might attend the recording sessions. Nelson Riddle was his favourite.

On June 30, 1982, we started recording. I was nervous—and for good cause. Because of the high cost of working with a forty-piece orchestra, I wouldn't be able to rehearse with it ahead of time, and we wouldn't be able to spend hours working on one song, constructing a few tracks at a time, as we had done with "You're No Good." It would be the first time I heard the arrangements Nelson had composed for me. We'd make three or four runs on each piece before moving on to the next, aiming to record three or four tunes in a three-hour session. I wouldn't have time to become used to the arrangements or tweak them to accommodate my vocal quirks. Furthermore, Nelson's sophisticated compositions demanded the flexibility to stretch and breathe freely across time, making it difficult to retake the voices later. I was going to have to do my live vocals again.

We began with "What's New." First, we ran through the arrangement for the orchestra's benefit. We began recording, and I sang the song three times. We kept the vocals from the first take. This meant that I ended up singing the song for the first time ever with that arrangement and in that key on the record.

My guitar skills were restricted to three-chord songs, so I couldn't accompany myself on such advanced material. To prepare for the session, I had to sing along with someone else's recording, which was in a different arrangement and not in my key. Joe Smith was right to be concerned. Fortunately, I was distracted enough by how much I enjoyed the music to stop fretting and just sing. It felt like swimming in cream while singing with Nelson's beautiful arrangements.

My courage began to fade as the clock spilled money and the temptation to rush through the songs pressed on me. John David Souther dropped by the studio, listened to a few tunes, and gave us positive feedback. I assume he was just trying to be kind, but I knew he appreciated the material and Nelson's work as much as I did and would notice if we weren't treating it with the attention and care it needed. John David's vote of confidence was particularly reassuring to Peter Asher, who, as a British, was unfamiliar with the material and had only encountered it in elevators. This had put Peter in the awkward position of having to work extremely hard to assist me in doing something he didn't believe was a good idea to begin with, all while working in an unfamiliar atmosphere. He didn't complain and went about his business as normal.

Now, if I'm in a store or a restaurant and hear one of those vocals I rushed through, it sounds like a sketch. I wish I'd had the opportunity to perform them publicly for a few weeks before recording them, so I could have filled out my phrasing ideas and sung them with greater confidence, but it wasn't to be, and I must accept that.

The next challenge was determining how to persuade my concert fans to buy tickets for a show that would not include any of my prior hits and would feature music from a completely different style and generation. I replaced my regular touring band with a lineup of seven excellent—in some cases, famous (bassist Ray Brown, sax player Plas Johnson)—jazz musicians, maintaining only the exceptionally versatile keyboardist, Don Grolnick. I was both honoured and terrified to be playing with these men. I added the Step Sisters, a vocal group in the style of the 1940s. My nine songs with Nelson weren't enough to fill out an entire concert. Singing with the Step Sisters also added a part of uptempo songs to the concert, making it a little more lively.

Suzy, my sister, had graduated from high school in the 1950s. She had gone to the senior prom three years in a row since she was a lovely and popular girl. She donned stunning waltz-length "formals" with fitted strapless bodices and voluminous skirts made of multiple layers of tulle. I adored those gowns, but by the time I reached high school in the 1960s, we were wearing sleeveless brocade Jackie Kennedy gowns to the prom. I felt I had been cheated. Jenny Shore, a stylist, was engaged to scour thrift stores for vintage fifties tulle prom dresses. In the show, the Step Sisters and I donned them.

On September 24, 1983, we gave our maiden performance at New York's Radio City Music Hall. I stood in the wings in my fluffy-skirted vintage prom gown, holding Nelson's hand. Nelson, who is generally upbeat, was just as frightened as I was. He gripped my hand. "Don't let me down tonight, baby," he told her. Then he drew up his jacket sleeve to show me the cuff links he wore. "You see these?" he inquired. "Rosemary [Clooney] gave them to me, and I always wear them when I need some good luck."

We started the event with only me and a piano onstage. I sang the first verse of "I've Got a Crush on You," and then Nelson and the orchestra rose from the pit on a hydraulic platform to join me for the refrain: "I've got a crush on you, sweetie-pie / All day and nighttime, hear me sigh."

The audience seemed to enjoy it, but I couldn't tell. Peter returned after the intermission to inform me we were a success, aware I was in a trance-like state of nervousness. Most performers battle with nerves on a nightly basis. I only remember the severe circumstances where time is twisted and I feel as if I am standing next to my body. This was one of those occasions. I was beside myself, as the term goes. I finished the second half of the play and returned to the small flat where I had lived throughout Pirates. I sat in my modest living room's window seat, where I could see over the Museum of Natural History to Central Park beyond. I knew that if the orchestra show was successful, I would no longer be restricted to the monotony of performing the same old songs. I had new old tunes and the Great American Songbook's mother lode at my disposal. I'd chewed my way free from the trap. I cracked a smile.

What's New, which was released the same month, sold over three million copies and spent 81 weeks on the Billboard album list. Rock and roll purists in the music press were perplexed as to why I had abandoned Buddy Holly for the Gershwins. The answer is that there was plenty of space for me to stretch and sing. Working in Pirates had honed my head voice, and singing standards allowed me to combine it with my chest voice to make what voice experts refer to as singing in a "mix." This gave me a newfound vocal flexibility, and I felt like I was finally starting to sing. The sophisticated sweep of melody and multiple levels of meaning in the lyrics allowed me to present a broader and more nuanced story—one that wasn't tainted by adolescent passions. Besides, I couldn't take the thought of such wonderfully crafted music being forced to ride up and down elevators.

There was another reason I embraced standards with such fervour. I never felt that rock and roll defined me. There was an unyielding attitude that came with the music that involved being confrontational, dismissive, and aggressive—or, as my mother would say, ungracious. These attitudes came at a time when the culture was in a profoundly dynamic state. Kids were coming of age, searching for an identity, and casting off many of the values and customs embraced by previous generations. This wasn't all bad; many of these things needed changing. (I was particularly glad to see panty girdles hit the trash heap.) Like the girls in the Weimar Republic of the 1920s who were liberated by their lack of dowries, I am happier to live in a world where birth control is readily available and a woman's right to terminate a pregnancy vigorously protected. Still, I cringe when I think of some of the times I was less than gracious. It wasn't how I was brought up, and I didn't wear the attitude well. Being considered, for a period in the seventies, as the Queen of Rock made me uneasy, as my musical devotions often lay elsewhere.

My candidate for consideration as the first fully realised female rocker is Chrissie Hynde of the Pretenders. She has the musicianship, originality, seductively cool attitude, and guitar chops to secure her place in the tradition. My crown, however tenuous it hovered above my head, is off to her. Singing standards gave me the flexibility to explore my mother's gentle nature, just as singing traditional Mexican music allowed me to explore my father's passionate, romantic side.

Nelson and I made two more records together, Lush Life and For Sentimental Reasons, but as we were finishing the third one, we discovered that he was going outside to lie down in his car during the breaks. He had become seriously ill with a liver disease and died after completing the arrangements, in October 1985. We did the final recording session without him. Some of the musicians were in tears, including his son, Christopher, who played trombone in the horn section. Listening to the last arrangements Nelson wrote before he died, I have no doubt that he was staring at his approaching demise and trying to fortify himself with the best weapon he had, which was his music. Nelson often said that an arranger had only a few bars in which to tell his own story: usually during the intro and sometimes a section at the end. The rest of the time, he was supporting the singer's story or fleshing out the songwriter's ideas. The beginning and ending of the arrangement for the song " 'Round Midnight" hold clues to what was on Nelson's mind in those final days.

Shortly after he died, I received a letter from Rosemary Clooney inviting me to sing at a benefit concert she put on in Los Angeles every year. I sent her a note that I had written with my fountain pen saying I would love to do it, and that Nelson had spoken of her often and fondly. She replied with a handwritten note inviting me to dinner at her house, saying she would love to hear about Nelson. I was dressed and ready to leave for Rosemary's when Jerry Brown came by unexpectedly. I told him I was on my way out to dinner, and he said he was hungry and wanted to go too. I called Rosemary and asked if it would be all right to bring Jerry, and she said it was fine. As we were getting ready to leave, Jerry noticed a large box of roses someone had sent to me sitting on the table in my entryway. Probably feeling a little sheepish about inviting himself to dinner, and being a person who is notoriously tight with a dollar, he picked them up and said, "We can take these to Rosemary."

"But they're mine!" I protested.

He shot me a mischievous grin. "If I take the card out, they'll be hers."

There was another reason for my enthusiasm for standards. I've never felt like rock & roll defined me. With the music came a stubborn demeanour that included being argumentative, unpleasant, and aggressive—or, as my mother would put it, ungracious. These perspectives arose during a period of significant cultural upheaval. Children were maturing, attempting to define themselves, and rejecting many of the ideas and practices of previous generations. This wasn't all bad; many of these concerns required attention. (I was relieved to see panty girdles discarded.) I prefer to live in a society where birth control is widely available and a woman's right to terminate a pregnancy is fiercely protected, as it was for the girls of the Weimar Republic of the 1920s, who were freed by their lack of dowries. Even still, some of my less than gracious actions make me shudder. It wasn't how I was raised, and it irritated me. For a while in the 1970s, being known as the Queen of Rock made me anxious because my musical interests were often elsewhere.

My pick for the first fully matured female rocker is Chrissie Hynde of the Pretenders. She has the talent, originality, seductively cool demeanour, and guitar chops to solidify her place in the tradition. My crown is now hers, no matter how shakily it hung above my head. Singing standards enabled me to convey my mother's gentler side, whilst singing traditional Mexican music enabled me to exhibit my father's passionate, romantic side.

Nelson and I collaborated on two more recordings, Lush Life and For Sentimental Reasons, but when we were finalising the third, we discovered that he was walking outside during the breaks to lie down in his car. He was extremely ill with a liver disease and died in October 1985, shortly after making the arrangements. The final session was taped without him. Some of the musicians were in tears, including his son, Christopher, who played trombone in the horn section.

Listening to the final arrangements Nelson wrote before his death, I have no doubt that he was bracing himself for death with the best weapon he had: his music. Nelson commonly claimed that an arranger only had a few bars to tell his or her own story, usually during the intro and sometimes near the finish. The rest of his time was spent supporting the singer's story or fleshing out the songwriter's ideas. The beginning and end of Nelson's arrangement for "'Round Midnight" indicate what was going through his mind in his final days.

I received a letter from Rosemary Clooney shortly after his death inviting me to sing at a fundraiser event she throws every year in Los Angeles. I wrote her a note in my fountain pen, telling her how much I wanted to do it and how Nelson had frequently and fondly spoken of her. She replied with a handwritten note inviting me to dinner at her house and showing curiosity in learning more about Nelson.

I was dressed and ready to leave for Rosemary's when Jerry Brown unexpectedly stopped by. When I told him I was going out to supper, he said he was hungry too and wanted to join me. I asked Rosemary if I could bring Jerry, and she replied it was fine. As we were getting ready to leave, Jerry spotted a large box of flowers that had been sent to me sitting on the table in my entryway. He lifted them and remarked, "We can take these to Rosemary." He was probably a little self-conscious about inviting himself to dinner, and he is notoriously frugal with his money.

"But they're mine!" exclaims the proprietor. I protested.

He smiled wickedly at me. "If I take the card out, they'll be hers."

CHAPTER 16

SUEÑOS

From Tucson, my father called. He informed me that Lola Beltrán, my favourite Mexican ranchera singer since childhood, would be performing at the 1983 Tucson International Mariachi Conference, which was in its second year. He asked if I wanted to go because I had never seen her perform before. I boarded an aircraft and travelled to Tucson.

Lola was fantastic. She controlled the stage as a tall, gorgeous woman with powerful cheekbones, her exquisite hands moving so smoothly that they were a show in themselves. Her outfits were extremely beautiful and well-made, and they were based on regional custom. She manoeuvred her peach-coloured silk rebozo into several stances with such grace that her small stage production appeared complex. Her voice was as powerful as that of an opera singer, but she used it in an entirely different manner. She sang largely in her enormous belt voice, but occasionally broke into a soaring falsetto, highlighting the break in the voice that a classical singer would strive to hide. This is a challenging tradition in Mexican singing, usually performed by male vocalists. Lola handled it with ease. She possessed an incredible dynamic range, ranging from a murmured, loving murmur to an agonising howl that could knock down walls. Her voice was fiercely sad, breaking through the linguistic barrier to rip your heart out.

After that, I was introduced to her. She gave me the peach-coloured rebozo after learning that I was also a vocalist. Later, while I was recording in Spanish, I wore it to the studio. It gave me confidence.

Her performance left me wondering where I could meet good musicians in Los Angeles that could play ranchera style and have the patience to let me hang out with them and learn. As a child, I used to sing Mexican songs with my family, although I usually only knew a few lines of the words and would hum and "La-la-la" through the sections I didn't know. Acquiring professional skill in this technique would be a steep learning curve.

While I was still thinking about Mexican music, I received a phone call from Joe Papp. In the fall of 1984, he planned to stage Puccini's opera La Bohème at the New York Public Theater. He asked me to play the part of Mimi. Wilford Leach was set to helm the film. Yes, I said. I didn't think about the challenge. I had adored Bohème since I was a child, having it played and discussed constantly at my grandparents' house. My grandmother had a tape of the Spanish soprano Victoria de los Angeles performing Mimi, which is still my favourite rendition. My grandfather would sit at the piano and play through the songs, with one of my aunts occasionally chiming in on an aria. It appeared to be family music. I was eager to get started.

Soon after, I was in New York with Randy Newman to make a television show about Randy and his music, which included Ry Cooder and me. We were travelling along Columbus Avenue on Manhattan's Upper West Side in the summer heat, on our way to lunch at the Café des Artistes. I enjoyed eating there since it allowed me to gaze at the Howard Chandler Christy murals of frolicking nude maidens on the walls.

A police officer sprinted past us at full speed, breathing heavily and attempting to catch up with someone we couldn't see. He pulled out a few yards ahead of us, and his revolver dropped out of its holster and fell to the sidewalk. We called him, but he was already out of earshot. I reached down to get the gun.

"No!" exclaimed Randy. "Leave it right there!"

"What if a child picks it up?" I inquired. "Someone could get hurt."

"Throw it in there!" he exclaimed, motioning to a huge garbage can.

"It might go off and kill the poor garbage collector," I contended. I resolved to take control of the gun and find a method to return it to the cop who had dropped it. After all, I was an Arizona cowgirl. My older brother, a cop, and my father were both expert marksman. As a child, I had learnt to shoot. Never mind that I am terrified of guns and support stringent gun control. Randy was no cowboy. He grew up in Los Angeles.

I grabbed the revolver and noticed two police officers driving by in a squad car. I raised my arm like a taxi driver and began waving the gun in their direction. Randy, who had firearms knowledge but was well aware of what happens to persons who point guns at NYPD cops, managed to conceal the gun while explaining to me as politely as he could that I was a reckless imbecile. He also kept us from making the first page of The New York Times the next day.

After some rapid negotiating, we agreed to stash the gun in my purse, which was actually a metal lunch box with a picture of Roy Rogers and his faithful horse Trigger on the lid. It was not a vintage lunch box but a reproduction that was a little wider than the one I'd carried in the third grade. The gun fit perfectly. We walked over to the squad car and explained what happened. I lifted the lid slowly and offered the gun in the lunch box as though it were a gift of the Magi. Miraculously, my head was not blown off. I looked down the street and saw the other police officer, minus his gun. He was looking anxiously along the sidewalk. This added credibility to our story.

We continued on our way to the Café des Artistes. Over lunch, I mentioned to Randy that I had agreed to sing the role of Mimi in La Bohème. He looked concerned.

"Oh no, little Mighty Mouse," he said. Randy called me little Mighty Mouse because I sang so loud. "That might be too hard for you."

I returned to my New York apartment and began rehearsing for La Bohème. I realised I should have insisted on auditioning for this play as well, because it was becoming clear to me how difficult the singing would be.

I expressed my concerns to director Wilford Leach, who had done such an excellent job with Pirates. He was used to his artists stressing over their shortcomings and encouraged me not to worry. He still didn't enjoy opera singing and was hoping for a more "natural" tone. We were almost there. Again, the rest of the cast was excellent. Wilford made them rely primarily on their acting abilities to tell the story, and they were up to the task. Rodolfo was sung to my Mimi by Gary Morris, a country singer with an unusually rich voice. His portrayal of the role was honest and poignant, and his singing was natural and unaffected, musically sure-footed, and appreciative to the piece's origins. The libretto had been translated into English by David Spencer. He handled it as if he were writing lyrics for Broadway songs, and I felt he did an excellent job.

The end result, which was released just in time for the holidays, was like a moving Victorian Christmas card. Despite the transition to English and the diminished orchestration, the story, which is heartbreaking, and the music, which is practically indestructible, were still incredibly striking. Instead of a complete orchestra, we had a small group of musicians who played flutes, guitar, strings, and a mandolin. It was intended to create a gritty, street theatrical sound. It was grim. The main issue, which I had no solution for, was that my voice lacked the training required for such a challenging part sung entirely in the higher extension. I foolishly assumed that if I could hear a decent opera singer, I could replicate the sound. I could mimic Victoria de los Angeles' enormous voice for a few notes, but I lacked the musculature to sustain it across a musical line. It was like knowing a few words in a foreign language and being unable to pronounce them correctly.

The reviews, some complimentary, some critical, lacked a rousing endorsement from the all-powerful New York Times. According to Frank Rich, a writer I much admire, "it's not consumption that's killing Linda Ronstadt's Mimi in the New York Shakespeare Festival's crazy-quilt production of 'La Bohème'—it's abject fear." He was spot on.

When Joe Papp came in to help out the injured cast, he was at his best. Whatever he said inspired us to keep working on our performances and perfecting them in the same manner we would have if the play had been a smash hit and headed to Broadway. "The work is all!" he said, before reading us a reassuring quotation from Puccini: "Critics are capable of doing much harm, and very little good."

I was able to relax and enjoy the rest of the run because I had been strengthened. I've always thought that failure teaches you more than accomplishment.

The disappointment of not being able to fully achieve a musical dream has happened to me more than once. The consolation reward for my Bohème experience was this: mastering the role gave me access to composer Puccini's thinking that the average listener does not have. Having the opportunity to be at such close quarters with music of that calibre was worth whatever personal suffering it caused me. The intimacy persists when I go to the opera house to hear Bohème in more skilled hands. I feel like I'm welcoming old friends I haven't seen in a long time and have missed when Rodolfo, Mimi, Marcello, and Musetta walk onto the stage. I am delighted when I hear them sing the exquisite arias in Italian with their wonderfully trained vocals.

I placed my New York apartment up for sale and relocated to the West Coast. My dreams at night were filled with the concept of a Mexican record. The dream worlds of sleep and music are not too far away. I frequently catch glimpses of one as I pass through a door to the other, much like meeting a neighbour in the hallway on the way into the apartment next door to one's own. In the recording studio, I would frequently fall asleep and wake up with fully completed harmony parts in my head, ready to be recorded. Music, to me, is dreaming in sound.

CHAPTER 17

CANCIONES DE MI PADRE

My Mexican fantasies had been strengthened by my time with Pete Hamill. He had studied in Mexico City and had an extraordinary comprehension of the subtle nuances of the Mexican art world, with a thorough command of Mexican literature, poetry, music, and visual art. Mexicans have a strong appreciation for poetry and utilise it frequently. It holds a prominent and ancient place in Mexican culture. The Aztecs termed it "a scattering of jades," since jade was their most valuable commodity, far greater than gold, for which they were slaughtered in large numbers by invading Spaniards. They believed that only poetry could communicate the more profound parts of certain topics, whether emotional, philosophical, political, or aesthetic.

Mexican song lyrics are rich in poetic imagery, from sophisticated cosmopolitan civilizations to the most primitive rural communities. I was learning the words to songs I'd loved since childhood and writing the English translations above the Spanish, so I'd know exactly what each word meant and could give it the appropriate emotional weight.

I was still looking for someone to start teaching me the rhythmic subtleties of the songs, notably the difficult huapangos, when I received another phone call from my father, telling me that the Tucson International Mariachi Conference had invited me to sing a few songs at its gala. The organisers offered me the famous Mariachi Vargas de Tecalitlán, with its director, Rubén Fuentes, to accompany me and make my arrangements. I was astounded! It would be like having Nelson Riddle and a whole orchestra fall into my lap if I sang standards.

Mariachi Vargas is a Mexican mariachi band that originated before the turn of the century and is largely regarded as the best in the world. Rubén Fuentes is a well-known figure in the Mexican music industry. He is a popular composer and was the musical director of RCA Records in Mexico for at least a decade, spawning a slew of ranchera recording artists, including Lola Beltrán. He has produced and arranged for Mariachi Vargas with Silvestre Vargas, son of the band's founding leader, since the 1950s.

This was a fantastic opportunity, and I resolved to learn three songs and figure out a method to rehearse them before travelling to Tucson to play. I chose songs I recognized from CDs my father brought back from Mexico when I was approximately ten years old. I'd heard them a lot but had never tried to sing them.

Rubén Fuentes went to Los Angeles from his residence in Mexico City to discuss the arrangements with me. Because my Spanish is restricted to the present tense and my vocabulary is that of a toddler, I begged my great friend Patricia Casado, whose family owns Lucy's El Adobe Cafe in Hollywood, to come translate for me.

Patricia and her parents, Lucy and Frank, were like family to me, in addition to serving the best Mexican food in Los Angeles. The Eagles, Jackson and John David, Jimmy Webb, and Warren Zevon were among the many young musical hopefuls who recorded in the studios near their Hollywood restaurant. Lucy was our go-to person for good food and supportive words. She was known to tear up a check if she knew a regular was going through a rough patch. Many journalists and politicians, including Jerry Brown, whom I met there while he was California's secretary of state, ate there and received special treatment from Lucy. People from the Paramount Studios across the street came for the food and the camaraderie as well.

On my way home from a tour, I stopped there on the way from the airport. It served as my home base.

I damaged my back a few days before Rubén came to Los Angeles as I was moving heavy luggage from the baggage carousel in the airport. I couldn't move and had to stay in bed. Cancelling the meeting was out of the question because Rubén had travelled a significant distance for the sole purpose of meeting with me. Patricia assisted me with styling my hair and finding a nice dressing gown. She assisted me in hobbling from my bed to the pink sofa in my bedroom, where we met. I was mortified to receive him in such a state, but I had no alternative.

He arrived with Nati Cano, who was the leader of Mariachi Los Camperos, a band closely matched to Mariachi Vargas in quality and based in Los Angeles. Rubén was in his sixties, handsome, urbane, low key, and I could tell that he was used to being in charge. Nati Cano, himself a brilliant musician and composer, would become my teacher and revered mentor for many years to come.

I showed Rubén the list of the three songs I had chosen. Two were huapangos, which, in addition to the complicated rhythm structure, require a lot of falsetto. He was surprised by my choices. "These are very old and very traditional," he said. "How did you hear them?" I told him I had heard them since childhood. "They are difficult to sing. Maybe you should pick something else." I wanted to sing the ones I had. He agreed to send the arrangements to Nati Cano, who assured me that I would be able to rehearse with the Camperos a few times before going to Tucson.

Nati Cano owned a downtown L.A. restaurant, La Fonda, where the Camperos appeared nightly. We rehearsed there in the afternoon, and I stayed to hear the show in the evening. In addition to the band, which featured one superlative singer after another, a pair of folkloric dancers performed traditional dances—"La Bamba" and "Jarabe Tapatio" being the outstanding numbers. I was very impressed by a particularly graceful young dancer, Elsa Estrada. Irresistibly charming in her beautiful white lace dress from Veracruz, she flashed her huge black eyes, heels drumming the intricate steps of "La Bamba": "Para bailar La Bamba, se necesita una poca de gracia." (To dance La Bamba, what is needed is a little bit of grace.)

Elsa had a bounty of grace. I decided that I wanted to put together a show in which I sang entirely in Spanish, featuring Elsa's beautiful dancing. I wanted it to be based on little vignettes of different regions in Mexico, much like my Aunt Luisa had done with her presentation of folkloric songs and dances from Spain.

The performance I did of the three songs I had chosen to perform in Tucson was rocky, but unlike my experience in Bohème, I felt that mastering the form was within my reach, and would simply be a matter of time and rehearsal. I found a teacher to show me the dance steps to some of the songs, so that I would be able to break down the rhythms and understand the phrasing better.

I asked Rubén if he would be interested in producing a record for me with Mariachi Vargas, and he agreed to do it. Remembering my unhappy experience with Jerry Wexler, I decided to hedge my bet and include Peter Asher as co producer.

When my record company heard my new plans, the people there were certain I had finally lost my mind: Record archaic songs from the ranches of Mexico? And all in Spanish? Impossible! I pleaded with them, arguing that I had sold millions of records for them over the years and deserved this indulgence. Peter was impressively game. He had never even encountered a Mexican song in an elevator, didn't speak a word of Spanish, and would be co producing with someone who spoke almost no English. I figured they were both gentlemen, and professionals, and would work it out. I was right.

Rubén Fuentes had been involved with Mariachi Vargas during La Epoca de Oro, the golden era of mariachi, stretching from the thirties through the fifties. I had grown up loving those records, mostly high-fidelity monaural recordings made in the RCA Victor studios in

Mexico City. They had a warm, natural sound, and I was hoping to capture some of that tradition on my own recording. Rubén was pushing for a more modern sound with plenty of echo on the violins and a more urban approach to the arrangements. I met with some resistance when I asked him to replace the modern chords with simpler one-three-five triads. Over the years, Rubén had been largely responsible for diversifying the mariachi style and cultivating a sophisticated urban sheen. To go back to a traditional style understandably seemed like regression to him, but I wanted what I had heard and loved as a child.

Luna, a very gorgeous black-and-white cow, had become a pet for me. Sweet Pea, her lovely calf, was born. I brought all of Luna and Sweet Pea's photographs and taped them on the wall at the recording studio. In my terrible Spanish, I joked with Rubén that I wanted more cows and fewer automobile horns in my arrangements. Rubén, who wasn't used to an artist expressing an opinion—especially not a female artist—was perplexed. To his credit, he made a concerted effort to reach an agreement. I didn't want to push him too much since I knew he knew who would buy this type of record better than I did.

The most difficult task I've ever done was learning to sing all those songs in another language with their perplexing rhythms. I didn't obtain the exact sound I wanted from the recording, but the people didn't seem to notice. Canciones de Mi Padre, which was released in November 1987, was quickly certified double platinum, sold millions of copies worldwide, and is the best-selling non-English-language album in American history. It was nominated for a Grammy for Best Mexican-American Performance. I was as taken aback by its success as the record label was. I must state that it succeeded due to the material's strength. The songs are powerful and beautiful, and they are understandable even to those who do not speak Spanish. Many musicians sing the material better than I do, but I was in a position to bring it to the world stage at the time, and it resonated with people.

I started frantically putting up a concert. I knew Michael Smuin, who had been the artistic director of the San Francisco Ballet for some years. He was a fantastic dancer and choreographer who created a fantastic production of Romeo and Juliet as well as an interpretation of Les Enfants du Paradis with an Edith Piaf score that I adored. He choreographed three short dance pieces for prima ballerina Cynthia Gregory to sounds from my Nelson Riddle albums, and I had the exciting privilege of performing them live with her. When I was on stage with Cynthia, I had to keep my eyes closed tight because if I looked at her, I'd become entranced by her dance, stand there with my mouth open, and forget to sing. Michael married Paula Tracy, a ballet dancer who served as the ballet mistress for several of her husband's ballets. She and I were quite close.

I wanted a stage director who could move groups of dancers around the stage while maintaining the integrity of the traditional dances. I also wanted a theatrical event with high production standards to frame the song and help an English-speaking audience appreciate it.

I contacted another close buddy, Tony Walton, and asked him to create my sets. Tony's film credits include creating sets and costumes for Murder on the Orient Express, Mary Poppins, and All That Jazz, for which he received an Academy Award nomination. He has designed a number of popular Broadway plays as well as numerous of Michael Smuin's ballets. The Smuins were personal friends of him and his wife, Gen.

I started putting together photos of what I wanted the show to look like, and Michael, Paula, and I spoke and dreamed together for hours. Paula had purchased a tiny wooden box hand-painted in black enamel with a design framed in pink roses and other multicoloured flowers while on a trip to Oaxaca, a state in the south of Mexico known for its art. I considered using the border design for our proscenium. Tony took that concept and added many fantastic ideas of his own, such as a gigantic fan that unfolded at the start of the concert and a moving train for a segment of songs about the Mexican

Revolution that I sang. Jules Fisher was hired as the lighting designer. Michael added a fogged stage filled with dark light for a dance he choreographed for a song about a ghostly ship with tattered sails ("La Barca de Guaymas"), and he also suggested releasing live white doves at the end of the show. Two of the doves had been taught to fly to my raised palms and perch on my fingertips. The dove wrangler told me to lavishly compliment them and tell them they did an excellent job. They didn't miss a beat.

I hired Manuel Cuevas, the designer of the cowgirl clothes Dolly, Emmy, and I wore for the Trio album cover, to create my costumes. Manuel had also designed the Flying Burrito Brothers' clothes for Nudie, the legendary Western tailor. Most people are unaware that the magnificent cowboy costumes worn notably by movie stars such as Roy Rogers and Dale Evans, Gene Autry, and Hopalong Cassidy, my childhood hero, are of classic Mexican design. Working cowboys in the northern Mexican states of Sonora and Chihuahua wear yoked cowboy shirts with pearl snaps. The styles were adopted by American cowboys, particularly in Texas, Arizona, and New Mexico. Cowboy hats and boots are also imported from northern Mexico and are still worn by working cowboys and gentlemen ranchers in the Sonoran desert, where my grandfather was born. The regional style of a person's attire in Mexico might tell you where he or she is from. Manuel, a Mexican native born in Michoacán, recognized that my ancestors were from Sonora and clothed me properly. That meant ultra-comfortable, hand-stitched cowboy boots paired with superb woollen cavalry twill skirts and embroidered cowgirl jackets. Manuel demonstrated how he would twist the thread while embroidering the design in order for the embroidery to catch the lights on stage. Manuel is the undisputed king of stage costumes. His rhinestone cowboy designs for Elvis Presley, Johnny Cash, George Jones, Glen Campbell, and others became iconic.

The mariachi's charro outfit is also an equestrian costume, but it comes from the state of Jalisco, where the mariachi originated. It's the tuxedo of a wealthy landowner who rode his horse to social occasions over considerable distances, his suit lavishly embroidered and his saddle, bridle, belt buckle, and spurs glittering with sterling silver fittings. When my sister and I were young, we fantasised of being whisked away on horseback by such a man, much like the heroine in Mexican films who is taken by her hero. When we went to balls and picnics in Mexico, my father stayed close by to make sure nothing like this happened. Mexican mores were still shackled in the nineteenth century, and girls were tightly supervised until they married.

After I started touring with the Mexican show on a regular basis, I would occasionally perform at a charreada, which is similar to a rodeo in which charros gather to demonstrate their animal handling talents. Music is included in the charreadas, and singers frequently perform from the back of a horse. The female competitors wear massive sombreros and long costumes with a double-circle fullness in their lace skirts, and they ride on side saddles. It is deemed unfeminine for them to ride astride. They are extreme daredevils, performing intricate acrobatics at breakneck speed with both legs draped modestly to one side, occasionally revealing a delicate laced boot.

When I was invited to sing at my first charreada, I knew I'd be expected to do so while riding a sidesaddle. I'd never ridden on one before, but my sister had, so I figured I'd figure it out when I got there. The first thing I did was inspect the horse they'd provided for me, a huge, attractive quarter horse gelding named Chulo, to ensure he wouldn't be frightened by the music. I requested one of the mariachi musicians to blow a loud trumpet adjacent to his ear. Chulo didn't even flinch. I clambered onto his back and nestled into the strange sidesaddle. I've always ridden horses, but a decent analogy would be asking someone who has always driven a car to drive the freeways while sitting on the steering wheel. Sidesaddle, I reasoned, was an anagram meaning suicidal. I was about to jump off Chulo's back and sing my songs in the middle of the arena when I noticed my reflection in a car window. My large hat and skirt, sidesaddle, and lovely horse produced a dazzling effect. Vanity won the day.

I rode into the arena and started singing. If the people in the audience like you, they will throw clothing at you at a charreada. Hats, bandannas, and hoodies began to rain on me after I sang a few words. I was afraid it would frighten Chulo, but he handled it calmly. The sound system started to feed back as we rounded the first corner of the arena. It was loud enough to bother my ears, and there were probably frequencies beyond human hearing range that were terrible to Chulo's sensitive horse ears. He began to shake his head and jump around, desperate to get away from the high-pitched shrieking. I tried talking to him and patting his neck to reassure him, but I also had to keep singing. I was wearing a body mike, which magnified my singing in Spanish but also my pleading with Chulo in English not to murder me by bucking me off and leaving me in the middle of the arena with a broken neck. I finally fixed the problem by directing him to the other corner from which the feedback was coming and stayed put.

I hugged Chulo after the show and thanked him for not throwing me off. I approached his owner and asked if he would sell him to me so that I could ride him in additional charreadas. The horse was given to the owner as a gift, and Chulo moved to Northern California to live with my other horses, Luna, and Sweet Pea. Unfortunately, he hurt his leg in the trailer on the way north, and we never got to perform together again. He retired and spent the remainder of his days wandering acres of lush pasture with other nice horses. I believe it was a welcome change for him, as the life of a working charro horse is difficult.

In San Antonio, Texas, we kicked off the Canciones de Mi Padre tour. We'd carefully advertised the concert as being entirely in Spanish, but I wasn't sure if people expected to hear "Blue Bayou" and other English-language favourites. The tour was scheduled to visit many of the same sites where I had previously performed with my rock band and Nelson Riddle. I wasn't sure how many people would show up. We were concerned since advance ticket sales had been slow. I was astonished, that night and throughout the tour, when I stared through the bright lights at the audience: the theatres were packed, largely with enthusiastic brown faces. I discovered that most Mexican audiences do not purchase tickets in advance, but rather come out the night of the show and purchase them at the box office. They also bring the entire family, including grandmothers and little children. The Canciones event drew a very different crowd than my past tours. They recognized the songs and sang along, particularly the grandparents, who had courted many of them. I was relieved that no one yelled "Blue Bayou" or "Heat Wave."

My favourite shows of my entire career were the Mexican ones. I'd perform two or three songs at a time, change clothes, and return in time to see the dancers. They never got old to me. The musicians were fantastic, and there were several outstanding singers among them. Every night, I learned from them. The members of our touring company quickly grew close, and I didn't sense the loneliness that I had felt on prior tours. Riding the bus late at night, I would fall asleep to the sound of rich voices speaking in a mix of Spanish and English, much like I had done as a youngster. After the odd experience of getting trapped in the American fame juggernaut's body-snatching machinery, I felt I was able to regain an essential element of who I was: a Sonoran Desert girl.

I released a second album, Mas Canciones, in 1991, with Rubén and Peter again co-producing. Paula Smuin, Michael Smuin's wife, developed and directed a simplified version of the play that included the dancers but was adaptable enough to perform in Carnegie Hall or at a state fair. I preferred the simpler version over the complicated one. We had enough production value just from the dancers' vivid outfit changes. Mariachi Los Camperos, my travelling band for Mexican shows for the following twenty years, had its own segment of the show and wowed the audience every night. They were the most traditional of the first-tier mariachis at the time, with smooth vocal trios and fantastic solo performances by Ismael Hernández, my favourite vocalist in the band. His booming ranchera-style tenor smacked the audience like a cannonball, leaving me stomping and yelling from the wings. My favourite memory from my travelling career is sitting calmly next to Paula at the side of the stage, calming my nerves while she cued the lights and started the show.

CHAPTER 18

CRY LIKE A RAINSTORM

I had discovered capabilities and sounds in my voice that I had never known existed after singing eight shows a week in Pirates, suffering with Bohème, touring with Nelson Riddle and the orchestra, and spending another year with the Mexican production. I was getting ready to record another English-language album and reached out to some of my composer friends who had consistently contributed intelligent, well-crafted songs. Eric Kaz, Karla Bonoff, and Jimmy Webb were among them.

I'd learned from singing so many vastly different types of music that there are an unlimited number of approaches to vocal production of sound, and that the majority of judgments about how to select them are made on an unconscious level. These decisions are made at breakneck speed in the brain's back room. They are informed by the story that needs to be communicated the most urgently and by how that story should be expressed. If it happened on a conscious level, it would take a week before the first note could be sung. I'd just sit back and let it happen, often shocked by the outcome.

When singing classical songs by composers like Puccini, the vowels become crucial, and the music travels on a big, open aah or o. With a standard tune, such as Rodgers and Hart's "Bewitched, Bothered, and Bewildered," one can race past the vowels and slam into the consonants without even braking. Beginning and ending consonants are quite important. In this way, the second half of the lyric to "Bewitched" is particularly rich:

Love is the same old melancholy sensation [plenty of sibilance and alliteration]

I haven't slept a wink in a long time [additional sibilance and a great firm k to slam against]

Jimmy Webb is one of the few modern songwriters whose songwriting craft is similar to that of the old masters like Rodgers and Hart, having the ability to construct a pop song with enough musical expertise for an orchestra to get traction. Toward the end of his masterpiece "Still Within the Sound of My Voice," he provides an opportunity to mercilessly pound an internal rhyme scheme:

And are you still within the sound of my voice
Why don't you let me know, I just can't let you go
If it's wrong, then I have no choice
But to love you until I no longer have the will
Are you still within the sound of my voice?

Jimmy Webb as a songwriter kills me. His songs are tough, but the emotional payoff is well worth the risk a performer must take in order to scale the enormous melodic range that his works explore. The payload of emotions is crammed into his chords and can elicit a strong emotional response in the first few measures of the opening, before the singer even begins. In comparison to another current master, such as Brian Wilson of the Beach Boys, he does not provide words that make it easier to achieve a lovely vocal sound. This is what gives his songs their grumpy appeal, whereas Brian creates lyrics that sing brilliantly. When I recorded his "Don't Talk (Put Your Head on My Shoulder)" and "In My Room," I discovered that his songs are not for the faint of heart, but they remind me of a beautiful horse that will give you the smoothest ride of your life if you know how to ride it. Jimmy, on the other hand, could scoff at any time. Jimmy's lyrics produce sounds that are consistent with his own vocal style: choirboy tenderness bolstered by a deep har-de-har Oklahoma farm-boy twang. I enjoy his singing.

When Peter Asher and I started working on the Cry Like a Rainstorm album, Jimmy wrote an orchestral arrangement for me of his mournful song "Adios," with Brian Wilson singing the complicated backing harmonies. I had known Brian briefly during my Troubadour days, when he was divorced from his first wife. He was always sweet and friendly, with no romantic motive. I found him at my back door several times, inspecting a small collection of money he said was ten or fifteen cents short of the price of a bottle of grape juice. He stated that he needed to consume grape juice in order to treat a health issue that was bothering him. He didn't say anything, and I didn't ask. I'd chip in the last ten or fifteen cents, and we'd pile into his gigantic convertible, the top always down, the back loaded with a sizable pile of Brian's dirty laundry. He seemed to struggle with his home arrangements as a bachelor, so I would advise a trip to the Laundromat, where we would fill a full row of machines. (I had an abundance of quarters.) After that, we'd sit in my living room and drink grape juice while listening to my little collection of Phil Spector records. Brian was a big fan of Phil Spector.

Under Brian's guidance, we recorded his harmony parts for "Adios" in the studio, with five different sessions of unison singing on each of the three parts, for a total of fifteen vocal tracks. He didn't appear to mind if some of the tracks were slightly out of tune, but when he returned to the control room, he employed the little "chorused" effect to combine the harmony sounds into the creamy vocal smoothness instantly recognizable as the Beach Boys.

Brian was making up the harmonies as he went along, but when he was having trouble working out a difficult piece, he would admonish himself and say that he needed to work at the piano for a while. When he sat down at the piano, he never performed any section of "Adios," instead playing a boogie-woogie song in a different key, quite loudly. After a few minutes, he'd return to the microphone and sing the portions precisely, without hesitation.

While working with Nelson, I became spoiled by the orchestra's massive auditory resonance and desired more of it. Peter, whose mother was an oboe professor at London's Royal Academy of Music, shared my passion. For many years, the recording practice was to record in small, empty rooms and then add electronic adornment in the form of echo and equalisation. I wanted to make a record with a lot of natural ambient room sound, and I discovered that on the large scoring stage at Skywalker Sound in Northern California, where I was staying, beginning with the album Cry Like a Rainstorm, Howl Like the Wind. The room, which was designed to record symphonic soundtracks for film, roared. It had its own particular sound signature, much like my favourite studios where I had recorded, most notably Studio A at Capitol. The room itself became a member of the band. I needed a large choir for two of the songs, so I enlisted Terrance Kelly's Oakland Interfaith Gospel Choir. George Massenburg's work on the title track, "Cry Like a Rainstorm," indulged our mutual enthusiasm for authentic high quality sound. It amazes me that almost no one listens to music in that format anymore since the development of iPods. We listen to music on crappy laptop speakers or in the secluded confines created by small earbuds, rather than in a designated place with enormous stereo speakers, sharing what we hear with others in the room. It saddens me.

Another item on my wish list was to perform alongside Aaron Neville.

When the Neville Brothers came to play in Los Angeles, word spread quickly. The musician phone tree would begin to hum. I'd get a call from bassist Bob Glaub or guitarist Waddy Wachtel, both of whom had previously played in my bands. We'd cancel everything and go hear Aaron, Art, Charles, and Cyril Neville play music that has only one place of origin: New Orleans. We'd wait for Aaron to perform his first major song, "Tell It Like It Is," and shout our hearts out. His scorching rendering of the mournful song "Arianne," which may leave me almost paralyzed, was a standout for me.

Aaron's countertenor register, as well as the five-beat West African rhythms that accompany him, are profoundly entrenched in the sophisticated eighteenth-century culture of the New Orleans Creoles. Children from wealthy families were frequently sent to Paris to be educated, and musical relationships with French opera were created. French Baroque opera tenors sang their high notes in the falsetto register or with softly drifting "head tones" rather than blasting high Cs from their chests as Italian tenors did by the late eighteenth century. Their melismatic vocal embellishment styles were regional and highly preserved. The Creoles spoke French and were Catholic. In modern society, their five-beat West African rhythms and falsetto high notes contrast sharply with the Protestant, belted sounds of rhythm and blues, which emphasise two and four (the backbeat) in a four-beat measure. (Think about the iconic Bo Diddley beat and clap one, two-three, one-two to grasp five-beat.) Aaron's singing technique has been compared to that of French Baroque opera composer Jean-Philippe Rameau rather than Wilson Pickett.

I'd never met the Nevilles because I was too bashful to navigate backstage politics and wrangle an introduction. I travelled to New Orleans with Nelson Riddle in 1984 to perform at the World's Fair. Plas Johnson, our Louisiana-born sax player, informed us the night of the event that the Nevilles were performing a late show at one of the World's Fair venues. When my performance was over, I rushed out of my costume and changed into a cotton outfit that would be comfy in the sticky New Orleans humidity. We loaded the entire band and members of the road crew into two cars and sped over to where the Nevilles were performing. I'd never seen them perform in front of a hometown crowd before, and they were pumped.

Aaron mentioned that I was in the audience near the conclusion of the concert and that he wants to dedicate the next song to me. I recognized it was "Arianne" as he began to sing! I was transfixed. He invited me to come up and sing with them after he finished the song. This is something I never do unless I know the person performing and have had a chance to rehearse with them, but after hearing Aaron sing "Arianne," I couldn't say no. I had no notion what I was going to do once I got up there. Aaron leaned forward and announced that they were going to sing some doo-wop. I was relieved because I am a soprano. I leapt on a very high portion above Aaron and clung on for dear life.

I awoke the next morning in my Royal Orleans Hotel bed, remembering the joy of singing with Aaron the night before. I thought our voices blended well, and I thought it would be fun to record with him. Then a darker thought entered. Of course, it sounded excellent to me. When singing alongside Aaron Neville, anyone can sound good. I continued my tour and shifted my focus to more feasible goals.

A few months later, I received a phone call from Aaron's management inviting me to sing with him at a benefit event for an organisation called New Orleans Artists Against Hunger and Homelessness. Aaron had founded the group alongside famed New Orleans composer and record producer Allen Toussaint and Sister Jane Remson, a charming, smart, and clever Catholic nun, to supplement the state's woefully inadequate facilities for the homeless. Whatever lingering grudges I repressed my early school experiences with the nuns at Saints Sister Jane's fiery charm and swift, empathetic approach to problem solving swept Peter and Paul aside. Sister Helen Prejean, also of New Orleans, is one of a small and determined group of Catholic nuns who, despite the church hierarchy's benighted and regressive attitude and best efforts to obstruct them, continue to undertake outstanding work among the least fortunate. They are my role models.

I flew to New Orleans with no idea what I was going to sing when I arrived. Aaron and I both went to Catholic school and have known Franz Schubert's "Ave Maria" since we were children. When my brother Peter toured with the Tucson Arizona Boys Chorus, he sang it as the featured soloist in shows around the country. Aaron told me that the song came to him during a time of great crisis and that he thought it saved him. He now incorporates it into his shows. We agreed to sing it jointly because we both knew the tune and all the Latin words. Aaron remembered asking me to sign a photograph for him, and I wrote, "To Aaron, I'll sing with you anytime, anyplace, in any key." We started talking about recording together.

I discovered four songs for us to sing. Two of these, "Don't Know Much" and "All My Life," went on to win Grammys. Aaron was scared at the Grammys and almost forgot about his most essential task, which was to thank his beloved wife, Joel. These occasions are frequently laden with anxieties and other unpleasant sentiments. It's nice to have one's work recognized, but rewards have never meant much to me because I generally feel like I know whether I've done well or not—and I frequently underestimate my own performance. In that case, no medal will make up for the sting of knowing I might have done better.

I hadn't expected to win a Grammy until 1975, and I hadn't planned anything to say. I went in search of the ladies' room after nervously thanking Peter Asher and having my photo taken by members of the press. Sarah Vaughan, a jazz vocalist, was slated to play at the Grammys that year, and I wanted to see her. Because time was running out, I dashed towards the women' room door just as someone else was hurrying out. I slammed my face into the opening door and spent the rest of the evening in the audience with a goose egg swelling on my cheekbone. Winning a reward means my name is called out, I get nervous, and then I get punched in the face.

Aaron asked George Massenburg and me to produce an album for him. He was determined to incorporate the "Ave Maria," which had special value for him. I recommended arranging it with a boys' choir because that's how I heard my brother sing it when I was a kid. We recorded at San Francisco's Grace Cathedral. I inserted myself as an extra boy soprano near the end of the song, harmonising with Aaron. People frequently comment on Aaron's angelic voice. In that context, he was the most powerful of archangels.

CHAPTER 19

LIVING THE DREAM

I had a fully matured voice with a vocal toolkit as diverse as it would ever be between the ages of forty and fifty, and I accomplished some of my best singing at that time. Among other things, I recorded two more Grammy-winning albums. Frenes (1992), which was entirely in Spanish, and Dedicated to the One I Love (1996), a record I made to help my tiny children sleep. I also released Trio II (1999) with Dolly Parton and Emmylou Harris, as well as Western Wall: The Tucson Sessions (1999), a duets CD with Emmylou.

During that time, one of my favourite projects was the recorded version of Randy Newman's musical Faust, based on the ancient German legend. When it was finally staged, it had a recorded cast that included Don Henley as Henry Faust, James Taylor as God, Elton John as Rick, an archangel, Randy as the Devil, Bonnie Raitt as Martha, a good-time girl, and me as Margaret, the ingénue who is devastated by Faust.

Randy's music can be depressing. To avoid appearing harsh, he will insert a shard of comfort so meagre that it appears Dickensian. His compositions are wonderfully composed, with a musical tension resulting from the juxtaposition of hope and complete despair. In his orchestrations, he may comment on the singer's narrative, using the instruments to convey jabs. Singing in the middle of one of his arrangements can feel like participating in a raucous debate, with people of varying intelligence, sensibility, and insight yelling and squabbling. He spares no one, and during recording sessions, he will make the orchestra faint with laughter, frequently with jokes about his deficiencies as a conductor. Whatever his shortcomings are, he manages to get the job done beautifully.

My voice began to shift once I approached fifty, as older voices do. I reworked my singing approach and sought new methods to express stories with the voice I possessed. Hummin' to Myself, my final solo release, was a collection of traditional songs recorded with a small jazz ensemble that featured cello and violin. Eugene Drucker, violinist with the Emerson String Quartet, came to perform on Alan Broadbent's arrangement of Cole Porter's "Miss Otis Regrets," composed for piano, violin, cello, and double bass. Drucker is a brilliant violinist, and as he took his violin from its case and began to play, the sound that erupted from his instrument astounded us all. "What was the make of the violin he played?" we wondered. It was a Stradivarius from Cremona, Italy, built in 1686. Of course, it takes a player like Drucker to make the Stradivarius sing so wonderfully. Roberta Cooper, a cellist of the Westchester Philharmonic and another outstanding artist, sat next to Drucker and played the cello. Her cello, which is also from Cremona, was made by renowned luthier Francesco Ruggieri and is a year older than the Stradivarius. I imagined the two instruments had met before throughout their long and risky trips through the years, and I wondered whether they felt like old friends reunited in the care of this extraordinarily skilled couple.

My final CD before retiring from singing was recorded in Louisiana with my friend Ann Savoy. The Savoys are a family with almost endless skill and abilities, and they are at the heart of the Cajun music industry. They live on a farm in Eunice, Louisiana, that has been in the Savoy family for seven generations. Marc Savoy, Ann's husband, creates the superbly constructed Acadian accordions treasured by Cajun accordion masters, of whom Marc is one. He's been constructing accordions since 1960, and when he lifts his enormous, attractive head to provide the downbeat for a Cajun music, he transforms into one of the great gods of rhythm and delight. Ann's friends will taunt her and tell her that she married the Cajun Heathcliff since Marc can be prickly and grumpy. He has a chemical engineering degree but prefers to work with wood. He could fling back his head and yell, "Let's all get drunk and roll in the grass!" Then he will astound you with his refined sense and courteous demeanour. I found him in a rare moment when he wasn't cleaning a bird, cooking blood sausage, or building yet another magnificent accordion. I told him that Ann and I had recently seen the Keira Knightly film adaptation of Pride and Prejudice, which had prompted me to read Jane Austen's novel for the hundredth time. "Oh," he reflected, "I just reread Persuasion."

Ann has alabaster complexion, black hair, the palest sprinkling of freckles, and dark eyes that slant down at the outer corners. She has a classic Greek profile with a Native American smirk on her face. She, like her husband, is an authority on Louisiana's Cajun/Creole cultures. She plays her enormous archtop guitar with a smashing rhythm and superhuman stamina, playing hour after hour for Cajun dances. She was born in Virginia and studied art in Paris. Ann can talk and sing in both Parisian French and Cajun French. When she isn't crouched over a guitar, you may find her at her sewing machine, creating a gorgeous frock to wear to the next dance or musical performance at folk festivals throughout the world. The end garment will be a 1920s design that will look lovely on her.

In addition to singing with the Savoy Family Cajun Band (Ann, her husband, and their two kids), she records and performs with the Magnolia Sisters, a group of ladies. They perform very old Cajun songs gathered by Ann. The songs are in French, with guitars, fiddles, and accordion accompaniment. The Magnolia Sisters have a haunting, plain tone, melancholy harmonies, and are especially lovely when singing in unison with no orchestral accompaniment.

Ann and Marc live in Paris with their two beautiful daughters. Sarah is a member of a Cajun band, and Anna Gabrielle is a talented visual artist. Their sons not only perform in the Savoy family band, but they also have fantastic bands of their own. These bands are made up of a younger generation of Cajun/Creole musicians who are dedicated to the tradition. Joel, a luthier who builds guitars, also produces and records in his Savoy farm studio. He is a Cajun fiddler and a Gypsy jazz guitarist. Wilson, his younger brother, plays bluesy honky-tonk piano and bawls Ray Charles oldies in French. He is a captivating performer. Ann's kitchen, living room, the yard where Marc is cooking something delicious over a fire, and the studio where the boys record are all filled with homegrown music.

When Ann and I first met in 1989, we learned that we had an astounding amount of interests. We had a passion for early-twentieth-century art, furniture, books, fabrics, and design. We even shared teacups on our shelf. Marc and Ann's farm life is quite similar to how I grew up, with family music and food rooted in regional customs constantly at the centre of significant activities.

After his death, my grandpa Fred Ronstadt's meticulous instructions for making a wagon or buggy were discovered in his papers: how to bend the wood, work the metal on a forge, and the finishing embellishments accomplished in excellent woodwork. There is also a description of his experiences "on the road," when he travelled to Los Angeles with the Club Filarmónico Tucsonense to perform concerts in the late 1890s. Marc's meticulous notes describing how an Acadian accordion is assembled, what he had to learn to make one, and why it produces an instrument that plays better than one made by a machine are fascinating and sound very similar to what my grandfather wrote more than a century ago.

Ann asked me to sing on her album Evangeline Made, which had current musicians singing classic Cajun songs. She flew to Arizona, where I'd relocated to raise my two children, and we recorded together, with Ann guiding me through the French lyrics. Recording our own project was a natural extension of our great connection. We'd both worked in noisy bands and wanted to pursue something calm and introspective. We wanted to sing about mature women's passions: love and concern for our children, love between trusted and treasured friends, the precariousness of romantic love, the difference between love for the living and love for the dead, the bitterness of a lost love remembered, and the long, steady love you keep for good.

Ann provided a fantastic array of song suggestions for our CD, Adieu False Heart, much of which was recorded at the Savoy's plantation in Louisiana. We chose the songs that made us feel like we'd die if we couldn't sing them. We slowed down Fiddlin' Arthur Smith's uptempo version of "Adieu False Heart," altered it to a lower key, and added a modal scale. We decided to record solely traditional music, and then did "Walk Away Renee," a mainstream tune from the 1960s. Ann discovered "Marie Mouri," a Cajun song based on a poem penned by a slave in the eighteenth century, and "Parlez Moi d'amour," a mournful song popular in Paris during the two world wars. We sat about in our pjs, rehearsed the harmonies, told tales about our lives and children, and drank pots of black tea and Marc's really strong coffee. When we finished rehearsing or recording for the day, we'd sit outside in front of a fire that Marc fed with boulder-sized logs, gazing through the woods at the moon or the setting Louisiana sky.

Someone once inquired as to why humans sing. They sing for many of the same reasons that birds do, I said. They sing for a mate, to claim their territory, or simply to express their joy at being alive on such a wonderful day. Humans, perhaps more than birds, hold a grudge. They sing to express how wronged they have been and how to prevent being victimised in the future. They sing to help themselves complete a task. They sing so that future generations will not forget what the current generation experienced, dreamed of, or rejoiced in.

The three most important aspects of singing are voice, musicianship, and story. It is a rare artist who possesses all three.

I was able to reconnect with the singing of Pastora Pavón, whose voice I heard rising from the 78 rpm records possessed by my father when I was three, thanks to the wonder of YouTube. She is regarded as one of the greatest flamenco singers Spain has ever produced, and is known as La Nia de los Peines, or the girl with the combs. It was thrilling to hear that voice again after nearly sixty years, and it was fascinating to explore the elements of a wonderful voice that could touch me so deeply as a tiny child and later in life as an experienced performer. What is it about her singing that makes it unique, scorching, and capable of crossing cultural and linguistic boundaries while addressing humanity's most fundamental yearnings and expectations? What is it that she has in common with her other European singing sisters, Yanka Rupkina of Bulgaria, Amália Rodrigues of Portugal, and Edith Piaf of France, singers who can grab me by the throat and demand that I listen to something they have to say, even if it's in a language I don't understand? I don't have an answer.

On November 7, 2009, I performed my final concert at San Antonio's Brady Memorial Auditorium. I was on stage with my favourite Mariachi Los Camperos and a fantastic folkloric dance ensemble, Ballet Folklorico Paso del Norte. My old roommate Adam Mitchell, a die-hard Camperos fan, was in the audience. We returned to my hotel after the show to laugh and reminisce about our Malibu days and how carefree they were in comparison to our mature lives, with children and obligations that we could only hazardly conceive in our hurried youth. Adam thought that of all the bands I'd toured with, some were as good as, but none were better than, the Camperos. He also believed that in all of the times he had seen me perform with a still-healthy voice, he had never seen me as joyful or calm as I was when singing the Mexican gigs. I concurred.